CHOCOLATE FANTASIES

CHOCOLATE FANTASIES

Live Your Chocolate Fantasies
While Savoring the
67 Best Chocolate Recipes in America

HONEY AND LARRY ZISMAN

POCKET BOOKS

New York   London   Toronto   Sydney   Tokyo

Another *Original* publication of POCKET BOOKS

POCKET BOOKS, a division of Simon & Schuster, Inc.
1230 Avenue of the Americas, New York, N.Y. 10020

ISBN: 0-671-63831-9

First Pocket Books trade paperback printing February 1988

10 9 8 7 6 5 4 3 2 1

POCKET and colophon are trademarks of
Simon & Schuster, Inc.

Printed in the U.S.A.

for
Jordana and Craig

may all their fantasies come true

How Much Do We Love Chocolate in America?

WE EAT

100	pounds every second
6,000	pounds every minute
360,000	pounds every hour
8,500,000	pounds every day
60,000,000	pounds every week
250,000,000	pounds every month
3,000,000,000	pounds every year

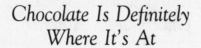

Chocolate Is Definitely
Where It's At

Craig Claiborne and Pierre Franey, two of the best-known and most-respected food experts in America, wrote an article titled "Chocolate Mania" in the *New York Times Magazine*. In the article, they definitively wrote:

"Everyone seems to have a never-ending appetite for chocolate."

"Culinary fads come and go, but chocolate remains."

"Americans are always going through tidal waves of enthusiasm about food. . . . Some of these waves crest and then recede, while others seem to get higher and higher. In this latter category, we would certainly place chocolate, the flavor that beats all others."

SYDNEY BIDDLE BARROWS
"The Mayflower Madam"

I am a longtime confirmed chocoholic—I would eat nothing else if I could. My fantasy, I'm afraid, is not terribly wild and outlandish but I dream of it constantly.

Kron delivers a 5 pound box of their dark-chocolate truffles and dark-chocolate-covered orange slices every day. The Four Seasons drops off one of their dark-chocolate mousse cakes twice a week. Fresh chocolate-filled croissants, David's Cookies (still warm), and slices of Princess Cake and Opera Cake from Eclair Bakery find their way to my doorstep every morning. Thick, rich chocolate milkshakes miraculously appear in my freezer along with chocolate mint Girl Scout cookies. And the very best, and most important thing is that I never gain one ounce from any of them. Every pound of chocolate I eat makes me look as though I'd spent an hour at the gym! The more you eat, the more fit and slender you become!

ISAAC ASIMOV
Author and Biochemist

I don't usually participate in projects of this sort, but I am a chocoholic and, as it happens, I do have a favorite chocolate fantasy. It is this—

I would like to be presented with a beautiful red-headed young woman in the nude who is covered with a thick layer of bittersweet chocolate. I then remove the chocolate as any red-blooded chocoholic male would.

Not practical, I admit, but a nice fantasy.

HELEN GURLEY BROWN
Author and Editor of
Cosmopolitan Magazine

My chocolate fantasy would be that I could eat all the chocolate in every conceivable form that I could possibly ever want and it wouldn't do anything bad to my body or my skin or my disposition. Actually it would have no calories at all.

TABLE OF CONTENTS

FANTASIES . . .
MORE FANTASIES . . .
AND CHOCOLATE FANTASIES

All of us have our own fantasies. Little boys want to grow up and be policemen and Wall Street lawyers specializing in mergers and acquisitions. Little girls look forward to becoming mommies and vice presidents of Fortune 500 companies. Taxi drivers dream about being Indianapolis 500 race-car drivers and practice when you are riding in the back seat. Struggling writers think about committing heinous crimes so their novels will get publicity, become best-sellers, and be made into miniseries on network television. And millions and millions of people buy lottery tickets each week willfully ignoring the slim chance they have of choosing the winning combinations.

You may not win the Nobel Peace Prize . . . break the bank at a casino in Monte Carlo . . . be the first person to walk on Mars . . . or record a heavy-metal album that goes platinum, but there are, happily, fantasies that can come true . . . and they are right here in this book.

On these pages you can delight in the sixty-seven best chocolate recipes from throughout America as selected in—what else?—the Chocolate Fantasies National Chocolate Recipe Contest.

These winning recipes include Cocomaretto Fantasy, White & Dark Chocolate-Raspberry Tart, Almond Fudge Brownies, Macadamia Mocha Cheesecake, Fudge Sundae Pie, Alpine Fantasy Fudge, Luscious Chocolate Bourbon Pie, and sixty more of the best in chocolate that the United States has to offer.

And you can make and enjoy every one of them.

What better fantasy can come true?

INCREDIBLY
SAVORY

CHOCOLATE FANTASY #1

Pillows made out of chocolate so you can have a bite of chocolate anytime you want during the night without having to get out of bed, turn on the light, and go searching for it. Sweet dreams, for everyone.

At the Chicago World's Columbian Exposition of 1893, the Van Houten company had so much chocolate and chocolate-related exhibits to display that it erected a stucco reproduction of a sixteenth-century Dutch town hall and called it "The Chocolate House."

The biggest attraction was a 10-foot high, 2,200-pound statue of Germania standing in a 38-foot high Renaissance temple. The entire piece was made of 30,000 pounds of chocolate, and it is believed to be the largest chocolate sculpture ever made.

In 1894, the "Chocolate House" was moved to Massachusetts, painted pink, and is now the home of a psychoanalyst.

No wonder all his patients have this unexplained intense craving for chocolate.

Chocolate fudge that is special . . . thanks to the cheese in the recipe.

CHEESE FUDGE

HELEN D. SOLES—CADILLAC, MICHIGAN

7½ cups (2 pounds) confectioners' sugar
½ cup unsweetened cocoa powder
½ pound American or colby cheese cubed
1 cup butter or margarine
1 teaspoon vanilla
¼ cup raisins
½ cup nuts
¼ cup coconut flakes (if desired)

Mix together sugar and cocoa powder. Set aside.

Place the cheese and butter in a saucepan or double boiler and heat over simmering water until melted. Remove from heat and mix in vanilla.

Mix together the sugar mixture and the cheese mixture. Knead with hands until mixture is smooth. Add raisins, nuts, and, if desired, coconut flakes.

Press candy into an ungreased 9 × 13-inch pan. Let sit until firm and then cut into squares.

Yield: approximately 4 dozen candies

Moist and spicy . . . not too sweet and great warm or cold . . . all the right combinations to please everyone.

CHOCOLATE APPLESAUCE CAKE

MADLYN CIONI—EAST PEORIA, ILLINOIS

1¾ cups plus 2 tablespoons sifted flour
¼ teaspoon salt
½ teaspoon baking soda
1 teaspoon baking powder
½ teaspoon cinnamon
¼ teaspoon cloves
¼ teaspoon allspice
6 tablespoons butter or margarine, softened
1½ cups sugar
3 eggs, separated
1 teaspoon vanilla
½ cup unsweetened cocoa powder
⅓ cup boiling water
1 cup applesauce
½ cup buttermilk
⅔ cup raisins
½ cup chopped black walnuts
flour
whipped cream

Preheat oven to 350°F.

■ 4 ■

Sift together flour, salt, baking soda, baking powder, cinnamon, cloves, and allspice. Set aside.

Cream butter. Gradually add sugar, beating until light and fluffy. Lightly beat together egg yolks and vanilla and stir into butter mixture. Combine cocoa powder and water and blend in as well. Mix in applesauce. Alternately add in flour mixture and buttermilk, beating well after each addition. Set aside.

Mix together raisins and nuts and coat lightly with flour. Fold into batter. Beat egg whites until stiff and fold in.

Pour batter into a greased 9-inch square pan. Bake at 350° F for about 45 minutes, until wooden toothpick tests clean. Remove from oven and let cool for at least 30 minutes.

Cut into 2-inch squares. Serve warm or cold, topped with whipped cream.

Yield: 16 squares

CHOCOLATE FANTASY #2

Chocolate fingernails for people who bite their nails.

An old-fashioned treat: toasted coconut goodness, dark rich chocolate, and a thick cookie pie crust.

CHOCOLATE COCONUT DREAM PIE

CAROL JOHNSON—WASHINGTON, D.C.

Cookie Crust (recipe follows)
2 ounces unsweetened chocolate
2 ounces dark sweet chocolate
3 egg yolks, beaten
¾ cup sugar
2 tablespoons butter or margarine
½ cup milk
1 tablespoon unflavored gelatin dissolved in ¼ cup cold water
1 teaspoon vanilla
3 egg whites, stiffly beaten
1½ cups whipped cream
½ cup Toasted Coconut Flakes (recipe follows)

Prepare Cookie Crust.

In a small saucepan or double boiler melt two chocolates over simmering water. Remove from heat and set aside. Combine egg yolks, sugar, butter, and milk in a heavy saucepan or double boiler and heat over simmering water. Add melted chocolates and stir until smooth. Add dissolved gelatin.

Remove from heat and let cool slightly. Add vanilla. Fold in egg whites. Fold in whipped cream.

Spoon mixture into Pie Shell and sprinkle Toasted Coconut Flakes over top.

Let cool before serving.

Yield: 8-10 servings.

COOKIE CRUST

> ½ cup Toasted Coconut Flakes (recipe follows)
> 2 cups flour
> ½ teaspoon baking powder
> ⅔ cup shortening
> ¼ cup ice water

Preheat oven to 400°F.

Cut flour and baking powder into shortening with a fork or pastry cutter. Add ice water, mixing well. Add Toasted Coconut Flakes.

Roll mixture into a ball and press into a 9-inch pie plate.

Bake at 400°F for 15 minutes, reduce heat to 375°F, and bake for another 45 minutes.

Remove shell from oven and let cool before filling.

TOASTED COCONUT FLAKES

> 1 cup coconut flakes

Preheat oven to 375°F.

Place coconut flakes on an ungreased cookie sheet and bake at 375°F for 4 to 6 minutes, until golden.

AND YOU THOUGHT THAT *YOU*
LIKED CHOCOLATE A LOT

Joan Steuer, appointed editor of *Chocolatier* magazine when it was first introduced, was the right choice. On good days she eats about five pounds of chocolate and, on bad days, only about one pound.

In addition to the usual mousses, cakes, napoleons, tortes, truffles, and candy bars, Ms. Steuer eats chocolate novelties like Monopoly sets, computers, tennis balls, dog biscuits, a Noah's Ark, a 5,000-calorie pig, a picture of herself, fettucini, pizza, and Merv Griffin's ear. She also splashes herself with chocolate perfume and sprays her office in New York with chocolate scent.

CHOCOLATE FANTASY #3

A home shopping network on television that only sells things made out of chocolate.

Who can resist oldies but goodies like doo-wop songs, '57 Chevies, and Congo Squares?

CONGO SQUARES

PAT POWELL—WINCHESTER, KENTUCKY

⅔ cup shortening
2⅓ cups packed brown sugar
3 eggs
2¾ cups flour
2½ teaspoons baking powder
¼ teaspoon salt
2 cups chocolate chips
1¼ cups chopped pecans

Preheat oven to 350°F.

Cream shortening and sugar. Add eggs, beating well. Add flour, baking powder, and salt. Mix in chocolate chips and nuts.

Pour batter into a greased 9 × 13-inch pan, smooth out evenly using wet hands, and bake at 350°F for about 25 minutes.

Cut into squares.

Yield: approximately 4 dozen squares

The tangy peppermint cream filling is the perfect spread for these brown sugar flavored cookies.

■ CHOCOLATE PEPPERMINT CREAMS ■

LUCY REAVER—LANCASTER, CALIFORNIA

> 3 cups sifted flour
> 1¼ teaspoons baking soda
> ½ teaspoon salt
> 1½ cups packed light brown sugar
> ¾ cup butter or margarine
> 2 tablespoons water
> 12 ounces chocolate (your choice)
> 2 eggs
> Peppermint Cream (recipe follows)

Preheat oven to 350°F.

Sift together flour, baking soda, and salt. Set aside.

Place brown sugar, butter, and water in a saucepan and heat until butter melts. Add chocolate and continue to heat, while stirring, until chocolate melts. Remove from heat.

Beat in eggs. Stir in flour mixture.

Drop by teaspoonfuls onto a greased cookie sheet and bake at 350°F for 8 to 10 minutes. Remove from oven and let cool.

Sandwich cookies with 1 teaspoon of Peppermint Cream in each sandwich.

1 cup confectioners' sugar
1/8 teaspoon peppermint extract
1/3 cup butter or margarine, softened
dash salt

Mix together sugar, peppermint extract, butter, and salt until mixture is soft and can be spread easily.

Yield: approximately 3½ dozen cookies

MEDICAL BREAKTHROUGH: CHOCOLATE THERAPY

Psychiatric researchers at Columbia University and the New York State Psychiatric Institute have observed that many of their lovesick patients craved chocolate and were soothed emotionally after eating chocolate. These unhappy people may have had an imbalance of phenylethylamine, a natural mood-altering chemical found in chocolate and in the human brain.

Phenylethylamine is identical to a hormone-triggering substance manufactured by the brain when an individual is experiencing infatuation, love, and passion. Therefore, eating chocolate produces the euphoric feelings of love and ecstasy.

Cola is hardly a traditional food identified with the 50th state but it sure makes a hardy and moist cake with universal appeal.

COCOA-COLA CAKE

ANGIE FREDRICKSON—WAHIAWA, HAWAII

1 cup cola
1 cup butter or margarine
6 heaping tablespoons unsweetened cocoa powder
2 cups flour
2 cups sugar
½ cup buttermilk
2 eggs, beaten
1 teaspoon baking soda
½ teaspoon salt
1¾ cups miniature marshmallows
Frosting (recipe follows)
nuts

Preheat oven to 350°F.

Place cola, butter, and cocoa powder in a heavy saucepan and heat to boiling. Remove from heat and set aside.

Combine flour, sugar, buttermilk, eggs, baking soda, and salt, mixing together well. Add cola mixture, stirring well. Batter will be very thin.

Pour batter into an ungreased 9 × 13-inch pan. Top with marshmallows.

Bake at 350°F for about 40 minutes, until wooden toothpick tests clean. Remove from oven and immediately cover with Frosting. Sprinkle nuts over top.

Yield: 10-12 servings

FROSTING

6 tablespoons cola
6 tablespoons unsweetened cocoa powder
½ cup butter or margarine
1½ teaspoons vanilla
3¾ cups confectioners' sugar

Combine cola, cocoa powder, butter, and vanilla in a saucepan. Heat to boiling.

Remove from heat, stir in confectioners' sugar, and beat well.

CHOCOLATE FANTASY #4

Flexible chocolate so you could always fold some up and carry it in your wallet.

CHOCOLATE FANTASY #5

Autumn.
The leaves turn different colors—dark, milk, semisweet, white—and fall from trees onto the ground where they are picked up and feasted upon.

LAW, ORDER, AND CHOCOLATE KUNG FU

A woman was leaving an ice cream parlor in Albany, New York, carrying a hot-fudge sundae, when she was confronted by a man who tried to steal her purse. In defense, she repeatedly hit him with her hot-fudge sundae until the man fled without getting anything.

These tasty little cookies have a coating of confectioners' sugar and will delight you as they melt in your mouth.

BOSTON BUTTER BALLS

BERNADETTE GILLINGS—MINOT, NORTH DAKOTA

1 cup butter or margarine, softened
5 tablespoons sugar
1 teaspoon vanilla
¾ cup finely chopped nuts
½ cup semisweet chocolate chips
1 tablespoon unsweetened cocoa powder
1 teaspoon cinnamon
1½ cups flour
confectioners' sugar

Preheat oven to 325°F.

Cream butter, gradually adding sugar, until thoroughly mixed together. Stir in vanilla, nuts, and chocolate chips. Set aside.

Mix together cocoa, cinnamon, and flour. Add gradually to creamed mixture, blending well.

Shape batter by rounded teaspoons into large marble-sized balls. Place on ungreased cookie sheets and bake at 325°F for 10 to 15 minutes, until golden brown.

Let cookies cool for about 1 minute and then roll in confectioners' sugar.

Yield: approximately 5 dozen cookies

Mashed potatoes in chocolate cake? You bet, and it is a new treat for anyone who has never tried it before.

MASHED POTATO CHOCOLATE CAKE

ELIZABETH D. KINKADE—ROCKFORD, ILLINOIS

½ cup milk
3 ounces unsweetened chocolate
1 cup shortening
2 cups sugar
1 cup hot mashed potatoes
4 eggs, separated
2 cups sifted flour
1 tablespoon baking powder
dash salt
1 teaspoon vanilla
Fluffy Frosting (recipe follows)

Preheat oven to 350°F.

Slowly heat milk in a saucepan. Add chocolate and continue to heat, stirring constantly, until chocolate melts. Remove from heat and set aside to cool.

Cream shortening and 1¾ cups of the sugar, mixing until light and fluffy. Set aside.

Combine chocolate mixture and mashed potatoes. Add to shortening mixture. Beat in egg yolks. Sift together flour, baking powder, and salt. Add to batter. Add vanilla. Set aside.

Beat egg whites until stiff, gradually adding the remaining ¼ cup sugar. Fold into batter. Mixture will be slightly thick and sticky.

Divide into 3 greased and waxed-paper-lined 8-inch layer pans. Bake at 350°F for about 30 minutes, until wooden toothpick tests clean. Remove from oven, let cool, and arrange in 3 layers with Fluffy Frosting between each layer and around sides.

Yield: 10-12 servings

FLUFFY FROSTING

1 cup sugar
4 egg whites
1 tablespoon corn syrup
⅛ teaspoon cream of tartar

Mix together sugar, egg whites, corn syrup, and cream of tartar and heat in a heavy saucepan or double boiler over simmering water, stirring constantly, until mixture is very hot.

Remove from heat, pour into mixing bowl, and beat by hand or with an electric mixer until frosting stands in peaks.

A creamy, rich frosting that is good on any kind of cake or cookie.

CHOCOLATE FRENCH FROSTING

ELLE BECKER—RACINE, WISCONSIN

½ cup butter or margarine, softened
6 ounces chocolate (your choice)
2 tablespoons confectioners' sugar
1 egg, beaten
¼ teaspoon almond extract

In a saucepan or double boiler melt the chocolate over simmering water. Remove from heat.

Beat together butter, chocolate, sugar, egg, and almond extract until smooth.

Yield: 1 cup frosting.

CHOCOLATE FANTASY #6

Neckties made out of chocolate so if you spill some gravy on them, you can just eat away that part of the tie.

"GIVE ME YOUR SEMISWEET, YOUR MILK, YOUR DARK CHOCOLATE YEARNING TO BE EATEN"

For the Statue of Liberty Centennial celebration on July 4th weekend, 1986, Paul Berthon, a master chocolatier in Paris, created a 14-foot high, 4,000-pound pure bittersweet chocolate statue of the Statue of Liberty.

The statue was made using an original mold found in the Louvre Museum, contained $30,000 worth of chocolate, and took M. Berthon and his two assistants 800 hours to make.

Made out of tempered chocolate, it is estimated that the statue will last for 20 years.

■ 19 ■

Great in the morning instead of a sweet roll, anytime with a glass of milk, or a late night nosh with a cup of coffee.

 # CHOCOLATE DATE NUT BREAD

DIANA EVERMAN—NILES, MICHIGAN

1 cup water
2 ounces unsweetened chocolate
1 cup chopped dates
½ cup chopped walnuts or pecans
1 teaspoon baking soda
¼ cup butter or margarine, softened
1 cup sugar
1 egg
1 teaspoon vanilla
2 cups flour
½ teaspoon salt

Preheat oven to 350°F.

Place water in a saucepan, and heat to boiling. Add chocolate. Reduce heat to low, stirring constantly until chocolate is melted. Add dates, nuts, and baking soda, mixing thoroughly. Remove from heat and set aside to cool.

Cream butter and sugar until light and fluffy. Add egg and vanilla and beat well. Combine the flour and salt and add, alternately, with the chocolate mixture, beating well after each addition.

Spoon batter into a loaf pan.

Bake at 350°F for about 1 hour, until bread tests clean with a wooden toothpick.

Yield: 12-14 servings

CHOCOLATE FANTASY #7

A true Chocolate Fantasies book: each page is made from a different kind of chocolate and perforated so it can be easily torn out and eaten.

Right from the beginning, chocolate was considered a gift from the gods.

According to Aztec legend, the loving god Quetzalcoatl traveled to earth on a beam of the morning star bringing with him a cacao tree stolen from the Garden of Life (Paradise) as a gift to man. The gift was a consolation for having to live on earth. He showed the Aztecs how to roast the cacao seeds, grind them, and make a nourishing paste that could be dissolved in water to prepare a chocolate drink called chocolatl. This drink would be served perpetually in the afterlife.

Unfortunately for Quetzalcoatl, he was severely punished by his fellow gods for introducing the sacred chocolate drink to mankind.

". . . I'm everyone's adorable and witty grandma and I live on chocolates and impossible coddling."

Katharine Hepburn, 1986

We always knew you were special, Kate.

When was the last time you had a really good three-layer brownie with a cheese layer in the middle? Probably not very recently, and now you can see what you have been missing.

ROCKY ROAD FUDGE BARS

MRS. FRED NEDERHISER—ELY, IOWA

> 2 ounces unsweetened chocolate
> ½ cup butter or margarine
> 1 cup sugar
> 2 eggs
> 1 teaspoon vanilla
> 1 cup flour
> 1 teaspoon baking powder
> ½ cup chopped walnuts or pecans
> Cheese Layer (recipe follows)
> chocolate chips (if desired)
> ⅔ cup miniature marshmallows
> Frosting (recipe follows)

Preheat oven to 350°F.

In a heavy saucepan or double boiler, melt chocolate and butter together over simmering water. Remove from heat and add sugar, eggs, vanilla, flour, baking powder, and chopped nuts. Mix together well.

Spread mixture in the bottom of a greased and floured 9 × 13-inch pan.

Spread Cheese Layer over chocolate layer. Sprinkle with chocolate chips, if desired.

■ 23 ■

Bake at 350°F for 20 to 25 minutes. Remove from oven and sprinkle with marshmallows. Return to oven and bake for 2 minutes longer. Remove from oven, pour Frosting over top, and swirl Frosting and marshmallows together.

Let cool until firm. Cut into 2 × 3-inch bars.

Yield: 16-18 fudge bars

CHEESE LAYER

 ¼ cup butter or margarine, softened
 6 ounces cream cheese, softened
 ½ cup sugar
 1 egg
 2 tablespoons flour
 ½ teaspoon vanilla
 ¼ cup chopped nuts
 1 cup chocolate chips

Cream butter and cream cheese. Stir in sugar, egg, flour, vanilla, chopped nuts, and chocolate chips, blending mixture well.

1/4 *cup butter or margarine*
2 *ounces cream cheese*
2 *ounces unsweetened chocolate*
2 *tablespoons milk*
3 *cups confectioners' sugar*
1 *teaspoon vanilla*

Combine butter, cream cheese, chocolate, and milk and cook over low heat until mixture is melted. Remove from heat and stir in sugar and vanilla.

When Jackie Leppia, a California homemaker, wanted to make special chocolate chip cookies for her husband, she felt that the chocolate chips then available were totally inadequate. So she went into business creating Fred's Chips—The Chocolate Lover's Chip, a blend of top-grade European and American chocolates. Fred's Chips come in three different flavors: bittersweet, dark chocolate mint crunch, and white chocolate.

The chips are named after Ms. Leppia's father.

A pudding cake . . . with dark chocolate moist cake on top . . . and a deep rich pudding underneath.

MIDNIGHT SURPRISE

ELISABETH G. PELHAM—WILMINGTON, DELAWARE

1 1/4 cups raw sugar or regular granulated sugar
1 cup sifted flour
2 teaspoons baking powder
dash salt
1 1/2 ounces unsweetened chocolate
2 tablespoons butter or margarine
1/2 cup milk
1 teaspoon vanilla
1/2 cup dark brown sugar
5 tablespoons cocoa powder
1 cup double strength coffee
cold heavy cream (optional)
whipped cream (optional)
ice cream or ice milk (optional)
chopped nuts (optional)

Preheat oven to 350°F.

Sift together ¾ cup of the sugar, flour, baking powder, and salt. Set aside.

Place chocolate and butter in a saucepan or double boiler and melt over simmering water. Add to flour mixture, blending well. Mix together milk and vanilla and add to mixture.

Pour batter into a greased 8-inch square pan. Set aside.

Mix together brown sugar, remaining ½ cup sugar, and cocoa powder. Sprinkle over batter in pan. Pour cold coffee over top. Do not mix in.

Bake at 350°F for about 40 minutes.

If desired, garnish with cream, whipped cream, ice cream, chopped nuts, or a mixture of these.

Serve cake in baking pan, warm or chilled.

Yield: 12-16 servings.

CHOCOLATE FANTASY #8

After you finish drinking your chocolate milkshake or chocolate ice cream soda, you eat the straw, since it is made out of chocolate, too.

Dr. Ruth Westheimer, answering a question about the connection between chocolate and love in her column "Ask Dr. Ruth," wrote:

". . . the taste of chocolate is a sensual pleasure in itself, existing in the same world as sex. . . . For myself, I can enjoy the wicked pleasure of chocolate . . . entirely by myself. Furtiveness makes it better."

MAGNIFICENTLY
OPULENT

With two kinds of chocolate plus added walnuts, these cookies are truly three ways delicious.

TRIPLE DELICIOUS CHOCOLATE COOKIES

CHRISTINE TOMASIEWICZ—OMAHA, NEBRASKA

22 ounces semisweet chocolate, coarsely chopped
5 ounces unsweetened chocolate, coarsely chopped
6 tablespoons butter or margarine
2 cups sugar
6 eggs, room temperature
1½ cups flour
¾ teaspoon baking powder
½ teaspoon salt
1½ teaspoons vanilla
¾ cup walnuts, chopped

Preheat oven to 350°F.

Place 14 ounces of semisweet chocolate, the unsweetened chocolate, and butter in a saucepan and heat over gently simmering water, stirring constantly, until mixture has melted and is smooth. Remove from heat and set aside.

Using an electric mixer, beat sugar and eggs in a large bowl until a slowly dissolving ribbon forms when beaters are lifted (about 6 minutes on medium speed). Combine flour, baking powder, and salt and add to egg mixture. Blend in vanilla and fold into melted chocolate. Stir in remaining 8 ounces of semisweet chocolate and walnuts.

Drop batter by heaping tablespoonfuls onto cookie sheets that have been lined with parchment or pieces of a brown paper bag.

Bake at 350°F for about 15 minutes, until tops of cookies are cracked, slightly shiny, and soft to touch. Let cookies cool slightly before removing from paper.

Yield: approximately 4 dozen cookies

One chocolate chip provides enough food energy for an adult to walk 150 feet. Therefore, it takes about 35 chocolate chips to move you a mile, or 875,000 to get you around the world.

And some people say there is an energy crisis.

The combination of chocolate and peanuts is legendary.

 # CHOCOLATE NUT GOODIE BARS

GLORIA LANGAGER—SISSETON, SOUTH DAKOTA

> 2 cups peanut butter
> 12 ounces chocolate (your choice)
> 2 cups butterscotch chips
> 1 cup butter or margarine, softened
> ¼ cup vanilla pudding mix
> ½ cup evaporated milk
> 1 teaspoon maple flavoring
> 7½ cups (2 pounds) confectioners' sugar
> 2 cups Spanish peanuts

Combine 1 cup of the peanut butter, 6 ounces of the chocolate, and 1 cup of the butterscotch chips in a saucepan or double boiler and heat over simmering water until melted and mixture is smooth. Spread mixture evenly in bottom of jellyroll pan. Place in freezer until hard.

Combine butter, pudding mix, evaporated milk, and maple flavoring in a saucepan and boil for 1 minute. Add sugar and stir until smooth. Spread over top of chocolate layer in pan. Place again in freezer until hard.

Place the remaining 1 cup of the peanut butter, 6 ounces of the chocolate, and 1 cup of the chips in a saucepan or double boiler and heat over boiling water until melted and mixture is smooth. Add peanuts. Pour evenly over cake in pan and place in freezer until hard.

Cut into 1 × 2-inch bars. Store in refrigerator since they melt easily.

Yield: approximately 2 dozen bars

A cup cake is more than just a cup cake when it is a miniature creamy silken mousse cake like this.

CHOCOLATE SILK CUPCAKES

BELLE ROEHM—SPOKANE, WASHINGTON

> 4 ounces unsweetened chocolate
> 1 cup butter or margarine, softened
> 2 cups sifted confectioners' sugar
> 4 eggs
> ¾ teaspoon peppermint extract
> 1 teaspoon vanilla
> 1 cup vanilla wafer crumbs
> 8 ounces frozen whipped topping
> maraschino cherries

Melt chocolate in a saucepan or double boiler over simmering water. Remove from heat.

Using an electric mixer, beat together butter and sugar until light and fluffy. Add melted chocolate and continue beating together thoroughly. Add eggs and beat until fluffy. Beat in peppermint extract and vanilla.

Divide and sprinkle ½ cup of the cookie crumbs into 16 cupcake liners. Spoon chocolate batter into liners and then sprinkle remaining cookie crumbs over top.

Place in freezer for at least 2 hours. Just before serving, cover with whipped topping and maraschino cherries.

Yield: 16 cupcakes

CHOCOLATE FANTASY #9

The Chocolate Emergency Service: a 24-hour-a-day delivery service to homes, offices, factories, or wherever you might be when the sudden urge for chocolate hits, especially late at night, on holidays, or during the weekends when many stores are closed.

A 12-ounce package of chocolate chips contains about 700 chips.
(If you don't believe us, count them yourself.)

Fudge Sundae Pie is a sumptuous dessert that is great on "Sundae" or any other day of the week.

FUDGE SUNDAE PIE

MABEL BOWMAN—OSCEOLA, INDIANA

1 cup evaporated milk
6 ounces your choice chocolate
1 cup miniature marshmallows
¼ teaspoon vanilla
vanilla wafers
1 quart ice cream or ice milk, flavor of your choice,
    slightly softened
pecans

Combine evaporated milk, chocolate, marshmallows, and vanilla in a saucepan or double boiler and heat over simmering water until chocolate and marshmallows have melted and mixture thickens. Remove from heat and set aside. Let cool to room temperature.

Line the bottom and sides of a 9-inch pie pan with vanilla wafers. Spoon half of the ice cream over the vanilla wafers. Cover with half of the chocolate mixture. Spoon remainder of ice cream over chocolate. Arrange pecans on top.

Serve immediately or store in refrigerator.

Yield: 8-10 servings

CHOCOLATE FANTASY #10

The banning of Chocoholics Anonymous as a subversive organization , opposed to everthing that is good and right in America.

AND EVERYONE THOUGHT
YOU WERE TAKING WORK HOME EACH NIGHT

The Executive Sweet of Bellaire, Texas, sells chocolate chip cookies packed in specially designed carrying boxes that look like briefcases.

Buttermilk makes this cake so moist that it does not need any frosting, and it is perfect for a snack anytime . . . even for breakfast.

BUTTERMILK SNACKCAKE

VIOLET DAILEY—PINE BLUFF, ARKANSAS

½ cup shortening
2 cups sugar
2 eggs
4 tablespoons unsweetened cocoa powder
pinch salt
2 cups flour
1 teaspoon baking soda
2 teaspoons vanilla
½ cup buttermilk
1 scant cup boiling water

Preheat oven to 350°F.

Cream shortening and sugar. Add eggs, one at a time, beating well after each addition. Sift together cocoa powder, salt, flour, and baking soda. Add to shortening mixture along with vanilla and buttermilk. Add boiling water, mixing together well.

Pour batter into 2 greased and floured layer pans or loaf pans.

Bake at 350°F for 20 to 25 minutes, until wooden toothpick tests clean.

Yield: 10-12 servings

Making bread pudding with a chocolate mint flavor is a creative variation on a traditional childhood favorite.

CHOCOLATE MINT BREAD PUDDING

ROXANNE E. CHAN—ALBANY, CALIFORNIA

2 cups bread cubes (any kind of bread)
1½ cups chocolate mint chips
½ cup crushed peppermint candy
2 cups milk
2 tablespoons butter or margarine
⅛ teaspoon peppermint extract
3 eggs
1 cup cream
Chocolate Mint Chantilly (recipe follows)

Preheat oven to 325°F.

Place bread cubes in a greased 2-quart rectangular baking dish. Sprinkle chocolate mint chips and peppermint candy over top. Set aside.

Scald the milk, stir in butter and peppermint extract. Let cool slightly and then beat in eggs and cream. Pour over bread cubes.

Bake at 325°F for 30 minutes until set.

Remove from oven and top with Chocolate Mint Chantilly.

2 cups heavy cream
2 tablespoons sugar
¼ cup crushed peppermint candy
½ cup grated chocolate mint chips

Beat cream and sugar together until stiff peaks form. Fold in peppermint candy and grated chocolate.

Yield: 6-8 servings

CHOCOLATE FANTASY #11

Chocolate shaving cream to make an unpleasant task a little less unpleasant.

Anyone who grows zucchini always has the problem of what to do with all those green things. Here is the perfect solution.

CHOCOLATE ZUCCHINI CAKE

KAREN RAAB—FLORISSANT, MISSOURI

½ cup sugar
1 cup brown sugar
½ cup butter or margarine, softened
½ cup vegetable oil
3 eggs
1 teaspoon vanilla
½ cup buttermilk
2½ cups flour

½ teaspoon allspice
½ teaspoon cinnamon
¼ teaspoon salt
2 teaspoons baking soda
¼ cup cocoa powder
2 cups grated zucchini
1 cup chocolate chips

Preheat oven to 325°F.

Cream sugars, butter, and vegetable oil. Add eggs, vanilla, and buttermilk, mixing together well. Sift together flour, allspice, cinnamon, salt, baking soda, and cocoa powder and add sugar mixture. Mix well. Stir in grated zucchini.

Pour batter into a greased and floured 9 × 13-inch pan. Sprinkle chocolate chips over top.

Bake at 325°F for about 35 minutes, until wooden toothpick tests clean.

Yield: 10-12 servings

CHOCOLATE FANTASY #12

Research studies at a prestigious Ivy League medical school have discovered that copious consumption of chocolate leads to permanent weight loss.

Chocolate contains many nutrients, including vitamin A, phosphorus, potassium, calcium, protein, iron, niacin, riboflavin, and thiamine.

Instead of serving just plain old fruit salad, perk it up with chocolate which, as everyone knows, goes with everything.

FESTIVE FRUIT SALAD FOR ALL SEASONS

GLORIA T. BOVE—BETHLEHEM, PENNSYLVANIA

2 large navel oranges
¼ cup chopped almonds
1 large banana, cut into ¼-inch slices
1 20-ounce can pineapple chunks in its own unsweet-
     ened juice, drained
4 ounces white or semisweet chocolate, chopped or grated
crisp salad greens
½ pint sour cream
1 tablespoon orange flavored liqueur or sherry

Preheat oven to 350°F.

Grate 2 tablespoons rind from oranges. Set aside.

Place almonds on an ungreased cookie sheet and bake at 350°F for 4 to 5 minutes. Set aside to cool.

Peel oranges and section. Cut each section in half. Combine with banana slices, pineapple chunks, almonds, and half of the chocolate. Divide into 4 equal portions.

Arrange salad greens on four salad plates and spoon one portion of fruit mixture onto each plate.

Using a fork, briskly stir together sour cream, orange liqueur, and remaining chocolate. Spoon ¼ cup of the sour cream dressing over each serving. Sprinkle with reserved orange rind.

Yield: 4 servings

XOCOATL—THE ORIGINAL AZTEC CHOCOLATE DRINK

The trade association of chocolate manufacturers in Switzerland commissioned several scholars to research the chocolate drink of the Aztec Indians and develop a recipe that would duplicate their original drink.

2½ ounces unsweetened chocolate
3 almonds, crushed in a mortar with a pestle
2 cups warm milk
2 tablespoons honey
grated rind of ½ lemon
¾ ounce dark rum
⅜ ounce arrack (coconut palm liqueur)
dash allspice
dash ginger

Combine chocolate, almonds, and milk and heat over a low flame until chocolate melts. Chill in refrigerator. When well chilled, place in a blender or a shaker and add honey, lemon rind, dark rum, arrack, allspice, and ginger. Beat to a froth and serve.

"Delicious little cookies with dark sweet chocolate and filled with pecans and walnuts" is not an exact translation of Lieselkuchen but it is a good description of what you get when you make this recipe.

LIESELKUCHEN

MARGARET GOUGHNOUR—PORTLAND, OREGON

4 ounces dark sweet chocolate, grated
½ cup pecans
½ cup walnuts
6 tablespoons sugar
1 teaspoon vanilla
2½ cups flour
½ cup plus 2 tablespoons butter or margarine, softened
confectioners' sugar

Preheat oven to 250°F.

Mix together chocolate, nuts, sugar, vanilla, and flour. Cut in butter.

Roll batter into small balls and set on an ungreased cookie sheet.

Bake at 250°F for 40 minutes. Remove from oven and roll cookies, while still warm, in confectioners' sugar.

Yield: approximately 2½ dozen cookies

CHOCOLATE FANTASY #13

By unanimous vote in a special joint session of Congress, it was decreed that the second paragraph of the Declaration of Independence is hereby amended to read:

We hold these Truths to be self-evident, that all Men and Women are created equal, that they are endowed by their Creator with certain unalienable Rights, that among these are Life, Liberty, and the Pursuit of Chocolate.

WEBSTER'S BROUGHT UP TO DATE

Definitions

Chocophile—a person who loves chocolate
Chocoholic—a person who loves, really loves, chocolate.

CHOCOLATE FANTASY #14

In a rare show of cooperation and harmony, all the members of the United Nations joined together without dissent to replace the present symbol of international peace and love—a dove carrying an olive branch—with a new emblem: a chocolate chip.

THE ULTIMATE IN "USER FRIENDLY"

The Chocolate Software Company in Los Angeles has programmed the Chocolate Byte, a 5¼-inch, 4.8-ounce "floppy disk" of milk chocolate that is hand molded by a little old lady named Gayle in Tarzana, California. A byte is taken out of a corner of each floppy disk.

The chocolate disk sells for $9.95 and, for real computer users, comes with a $1.00 rebate coupon for Memorex computer products, including computer paper and, of course, floppy disks.

The marshmallow creme makes these brownies undisputed winners.

PATTIE'S NEVER FAIL BROWNIES

BRIDGET G. SMART—SAN ANTONIO, TEXAS

1 cup sugar
½ cup plus 2 tablespoons butter or margarine, softened
2 eggs
6 tablespoons unsweetened cocoa powder
½ cup flour
1 teaspoon vanilla
½ cup chopped nuts
½ to 1 cup marshmallow creme

Preheat oven to 325°F.

Cream together sugar and butter. Add eggs, beating well. Mix in cocoa powder, flour, and vanilla. Stir in nuts.

Pour batter into a greased 8-inch square pan. Swirl marshmallow cream into batter in all directions.

Bake at 325°F for 30 to 35 minutes, until brownies test clean with a wooden toothpick.

Cut into 2-inch squares.

Yield: 16 brownies

Tired of coffee and tea for breakfast? Switch to Mug O'The Morn' and you will have a real incentive to get out of bed every day.

MUG O'THE MORN' CHOCOLATE MOCHA COFFEE

H. MARCELLA COLLINS—VENTURA, CALIFORNIA

2 heaping teaspoons cocoa mix
dash ginger
¼ teaspoon cinnamon
1½ cups hot brewed coffee
milk or cream (if desired)

Put cocoa mix, ginger, and cinnamon in a mug. Pour in coffee, stirring well. Add milk, if desired.

Yield: 1 mug.

Baker's chocolate is not called so because it is used in cooking. It is named after Dr. James Baker, who provided financial support to an early chocolate maker in the United States.

WONDROUSLY
ENTICING

Prunes and cognac may not be an everyday combination but together here they make a delightfully moist cake topped with a thick glaze.

CHOCOLATE, PRUNE, AND COGNAC CAKE

LAURA BEHLER—SPRING, TEXAS

¾ pound soft-pack pitted prunes, cut into raisin-sized
    pieces
⅓ cup plus 5 tablespoons cognac or brandy
1 cup plus 3 tablespoons sugar
9 ounces chocolate (your choice)
2 teaspoons instant coffee powder
¾ cup plus 2 tablespoons butter or margarine
¾ cup plus 2 tablespoons flour
1 teaspoon cinnamon
¾ teaspoon allspice
5 eggs at room temperature, separated
dash salt
dash cream of tartar
Chocolate Glaze (recipe follows)

Combine prunes, ⅓ cup cognac, and 3 tablespoons sugar in a small heavy saucepan and heat to a simmer, stirring constantly. Remove from heat and let steep for 2 hours.

Melt chocolate with remaining 5 tablespoons cognac and coffee powder in a 2-quart saucepan over low heat, stirring constantly. Add butter, 1 tablespoon at a time. Mix in ¾ cup of the sugar, flour, cinnamon, and allspice. Blend in egg yolks and remove from heat. Let mixture cool slightly.

Preheat oven to 350°F.

Using mixer, beat egg whites, salt, and cream of tartar until soft peaks form. Add remaining ¼ cup sugar, 1 tablespoon at a time, and beat until almost stiff but not dry.

Whisk chocolate mixture to loosen and gently fold in ¼ of the egg white mixture. Fold mixture back into remaining egg whites. Gently fold in prunes. Pour into a bundt pan that has been buttered and dusted with flour.

Bake at 350°F for about 1 hour, until center is firm to touch. Remove from oven and let cool for 25 minutes, invert cake onto rack, and cool completely. Wrap tightly and let stand at room temperature overnight.

Spoon Glaze over cake, allowing some to drip down sides. Let stand until set.

Yield: 10-12 servings

GLAZE

> ¼ *cup milk*
> 4½ *ounces chocolate (your choice)*
> 3 *tablespoons cognac or brandy*

Simmer milk, remove from heat, and stir in chocolate. Cover and let stand for 5 minutes. Add cognac.

Let cool until glaze mounds slightly on spoon.

An old reliable recipe that is easy to make, never fails, and, of course, is truly delicious.

CHOCOLATE FUDGE PLUS

JENNIE N. COTTON—WILMINGTON, DELAWARE

2¼ cups sugar
¾ cup evaporated milk
⅓ cup light corn syrup
2 tablespoons butter or margarine
12 ounces chocolate (your choice)
1 teaspoon vanilla
1 cup raisins, coconut flakes, or nuts, or a combination

Combine sugar, milk, corn syrup, and butter in a large heavy saucepan. Bring to a boil over medium heat, stirring constantly, and continue cooking for 5 minutes more, still stirring constantly.

Remove from heat, add chocolate and vanilla, and stir until mixture is smooth. Add raisins, coconut, and/or nuts.

Pour mixture into a greased 9 × 13-inch pan. Chill in refrigerator until firm.

Cut into squares.

Yield: approximately 4 dozen candies

TIME MAGAZINE'S MAN OF THE YEAR FOR 1765

The man: John Hannon, an Irish immigrant.
The year: 1765.
The place: the corner of a factory in Dorchester, Mass., just outside of Boston.
The great event: the first chocolate is made in America.

CHOCOLATE FANTASY #15

A pair of spigots in the kitchen: one for semisweet chocolate, the other for milk chocolate.

Deep smooth chocolate filling in a light cream cheese crust . . . how could you go wrong?

CHOCO-CREAM CHEESE PIE

MABLE TAYLOR—KNOXVILLE, TENNESSEE

Pie Crust (recipe follows)
¾ cup flour
¼ cup unsweetened cocoa powder
1 cup sugar
2½ cups milk
3 eggs, beaten
2 tablespoons butter or margarine
2 teaspoons vanilla
½ cup chopped walnuts
whipped cream or frozen whipped topping
maraschino cherries
chopped nuts

Prepare Pie Crust.

Place flour, cocoa powder, and sugar in a saucepan. Stir in milk, eggs, and butter. Cook on low heat, stirring constantly, until mixture becomes very thick. Remove from heat and add vanilla. Add walnuts. Pour into Pie Crust and let cool.

Garnish with whipped cream, maraschino cherries, and chopped nuts.

Yield: 8-10 servings

3 ounces cream cheese, softened
½ cup butter or margarine, softened
1 cup flour

Preheat oven to 350°F.

Mix together cream cheese, butter, and flour and chill in refrigerator for 1 hour.

Do not roll out crust but, using fingers, press crust into pie pan.

Bake at 350°F for about 20 minutes, until light brown.

CHOCOLATE FANTASY #16

Finding out that you are a long-lost direct descendant of Milton H. Hershey, founder of the Hershey Chocolate Company.

Look—a crunchy topping of oatmeal and pecan pebbles afloat on a sea of chocolate.

CHOCOLATE PECAN OATMEAL SQUARES

SANDRA P, BERLINSKY—CRANSTON, RHODE ISLAND

½ cup sweet butter or sweet margarine, softened
½ cup packed light brown sugar
⅓ cup sugar
1 egg
1½ teaspoons vanilla
⅔ cup flour
2 cups quick cooking oatmeal
6 ounces (your choice) chocolate
½ cup cream
½ cup pecans, chopped

Preheat oven to 350°F.

Cream butter and sugars until light and fluffy. Beat in egg and 1 teaspoon of the vanilla. Stir in flour and oatmeal.

Press ⅔ of the batter evenly on the bottom of a greased 9-inch square baking pan.

Combine chocolate and cream in a saucepan and heat over medium heat, stirring constantly, until chocolate is melted and mixture is smooth.

Remove from heat, stir in remaining ½ teaspoon of vanilla, and spread over batter in baking pan. Mix nuts into remaining oatmeal batter and sprinkle over chocolate in baking pan. Mixture will look like small pebbles in the middle of a sea of chocolate.

Bake at 350°F for about 30 minutes, until golden. Remove from oven and cool in pan. Cut into 1½ inch squares.

Yield: 36 squares

After a minor confrontation in a traffic jam at the entrance to the Lincoln Tunnel going from New Jersey into Manhattan, the driver of a Volkswagen found himself being pelted with a barrage of chocolate chips hurled by the driver of a black stretch Cadillac limousine.

The only injuries suffered were tiny brown spots left on the trunk of the VW.

Any cow would be proud to have her milk become part of this cool, creamy drink that gives new meaning to the word shake.

◼ CHOCOLATE ENCHANTING SHAKE

ROBERTA HANSEN—SALT LAKE CITY, UTAH

> 5 scoops chocolate ice cream or ice milk
> ½ cups milk
> 2 tablespoons chocolate syrup
> 1 tablespoon malted milk powder
> pinch nutmeg

Place ice cream, milk, chocolate syrup, malted milk powder, and nutmeg in a blender and blend for 10 to 20 seconds until smooth.

Yield: 2 servings

Forget the Book of the Month Club. Now for a mere 1,987 dollars you can get a lifetime membership in The Fanny Farmer Chocolate of the Month Club. The company estimates that an average 28-year-old club member would receive 480 pounds of candy over the course of his or her membership. The 1,600,000 calories he or she would consume could be burned off swimming from Miami to London.

Simple to make . . . fun to eat . . . chewy and crunchy . . . and you better make a double batch because they go fast.

CORN FLAKE CHOCOLATE SQUARES

MRS. HERBERT MAX—WEST HARTFORD, CONNECTICUT

½ cup corn syrup
⅓ cup brown sugar
2 tablespoons peanut butter
3 ounces chocolate (your choice)
6 cups corn flake cereal

Place corn syrup, sugar, and peanut butter in a saucepan and bring to a boil. Lower heat and add chocolate and continue cooking until chocolate melts. Remove from heat. Add corn flake cereal and stir to coat well.

Spoon mixture into a greased 9 × 13-inch pan and press down.

Let cool and then cut into 2-inch squares. Freezes very well.

Yield: approximately 2 dozen squares

Here is a rich French cake that is almost like fudge itself—a grand finale for an elegant dinner.

CHOCOLATE LOVER'S DREAM CAKE

MARIE K. STRAITON—AUBURN, ALABAMA

5 ounces semisweet chocolate
⅔ cup butter or margarine, softened
¾ cup sugar
3 eggs, separated
⅔ cup flour
¼ cup milk
½ teaspoon vanilla
⅔ cup blanched whole almonds, finely ground
½ teaspoon salt
Icing (recipe follows)
sliced almonds

Preheat oven to 350°F.

In a saucepan or double boiler melt the chocolate over simmering water. Remove from heat. In a large bowl, using an electric mixer, cream butter at medium speed until smooth. Gradually add sugar, 2 tablespoons at a time, beating until light and fluffy. Add egg yolks, beating until very light. Add chocolate, mixing together well.

At low speed, add flour and milk, alternately, beginning and ending with flour. Stir in vanilla and half of the ground almonds. Set aside.

In a small mixing bowl, using clean beaters, beat egg whites and salt at high speed until stiff peaks form.

With a wire whisk, using an over-and-over motion, gently fold egg whites into batter, just until combined.

Spoon batter evenly into a lightly greased 9-inch springform pan.

Bake at 350°F for 25 to 30 minutes, until a wooden toothpick tests clean.

Cool in pan on wire rack for 10 minutes. With spatula, loosen edges, and return cake, still in pan, to rack and let sit until cool.

Remove cake from pan onto serving dish and cover top and sides with Icing. Sprinkle remaining ground almonds over top and decorate sides with sliced almonds.

Yield: 10-12 servings

ICING

5 ounces semisweet chocolate
3 tablespoons milk
¼ cup butter or margarine
1 cup confectioners' sugar
¼ teaspoon almond extract

In a saucepan or double boiler melt chocolate with milk and butter over simmering water.

Remove from heat and add sugar and almond extract. Beat until smooth.

Hot or cold, this chocolate bread pudding is a major event thanks to the almond cream sauce.

CHOCOLATE BREAD PUDDING WITH ALMOND CREAM SAUCE

NELLIE TROSCLAIR—MARRERO, LOUISIANA

10 slices stale French bread, cut into cubes
½ cup condensed milk
¼ cup butter or margarine
2 ounces unsweetened chocolate
1 cup sugar
3 tablespoons unsweetened cocoa powder
1 teaspoon baking powder
¼ teaspoon salt
¼ cup milk
1 teaspoon vanilla
¾ cup chopped pecans
1 tablespoon brown sugar
Almond Cream Sauce (recipe follows)

Preheat oven to 350°F.

Soak bread cubes in condensed milk. Set aside.

Place butter and chocolate in a saucepan or double boiler and melt over simmering water. Set aside.

In a mixing bowl, combine bread cubes, sugar, cocoa powder, baking powder, and salt. Add milk, chocolate mixture, vanilla pecans, and brown sugar. Mix well.

■ 62 ■

Pour mixture into a 9-inch square baking pan and bake at 350°F for 50 to 60 minutes.

While pudding is still hot, spoon into serving bowls and top with Almond Cream Sauce. Pudding can also be served cold.

Yield: 6-8 servings

ALMOND CREAM SAUCE

2 cups whipped cream
1 teaspoon amaretto liqueur
1 teaspoon almond extract

Blend together whipped cream, amaretto liqueur, and almond extract.

CHOCOLATE FANTASY #17

A hot tub filled with warm, churning, soothing dark chocolate.

For $30.00, Rowe-Manse Emporium, a specialty store in Clifton, New Jersey, will send a bouquet of one dozen beautifully sculpted, long-stemmed, 18-inch chocolate roses anywhere you want to anyone you want. The flowers are made from milk or dark chocolate and come complete with chocolate leaves. The bouquet is wrapped in white tissue paper and sent nestled in a beribboned, gold-seal florist's box. A personal card can be included.

The chocolate factory built by the Hershey Chocolate Company in Hershey, Pennsylvania, in 1903-1905 covered 2 million square feet making it the largest such factory ever built.

This white fudge will bring visions of the snow-covered Alpine mountains of Europe and a unique continental taste that is so different from the dark chocolate fudge that is usually made.

ALPINE FANTASY FUDGE

DONNA LAMB—STAFFORD, TEXAS

> 3 cups sugar
> 1/4 cup butter or margarine
> 2/3 cup evaporated milk
> 12 ounces white chocolate
> 2 1/4 cups marshmallow creme
> 1/2 cup chopped nuts
> 1 1/4 teaspoons vanilla

Combine sugar, butter, and evaporated milk in a saucepan and heat to boiling, stirring constantly. Continue cooking for 5 minutes more over medium heat, stirring constantly.

Remove from heat, stir in chocolate, and continue stirring until chocolate is completely melted. Add marshmallow creme, nuts, and vanilla. Stir until well blended.

Pour into a greased 9 × 13-inch pan. Let cool and then cut into squares.

Yield: approximately 4 dozen squares

Even if you have a favorite brownie recipe, this one will still go to the top of your list.

MOCHA BROWNIES

RUTH RUBIN—WEST PALM BEACH, FLORIDA

½ cup butter or margarine
6 ounces semisweet chocolate
1 ounce unsweetened chocolate
1 heaping tablespoon instant coffee powder
3 eggs
1 cup sugar
1 cup flour
2 teaspoons vanilla
dash salt
1 cup walnuts

Preheat oven to 350°F.

In a heavy saucepan or double boiler melt butter and chocolates over simmering water. Stir in coffee powder and set aside.

Beat together eggs and sugar. Add flour, vanilla, salt, walnuts, and chocolate mixture, stirring together well.

Pour batter into a greased 9 × 13-inch pan and bake at 350°F for 20 to 30 minutes, until wooden toothpick tests clean.

Let cool and cut into squares.

Yield: approximately 2 dozen brownies

CHOCOLATE FANTASY #18

An all-expenses-paid week vacation at Club Choc, operated by Club Med, offering chocolate meals, chocolate games, and even chocolate sex, whatever that is.

Dr. Victor Syrmis, a child psychiatrist in New York City, received patent number 4,455,320 for a method of reproducing the image of a person's face in chocolate candy. His company, very appropriately called Chocolate Photos, makes boxes of bite-sized chocolates, each one fashioned after the face of your choice.

These unusual delicate crispy cookies with an orange-chocolate flavor are delicious by themselves . . . and perfect served with a cool dish of ice cream or sherbet.

CHOCOLATE FANS

VIRGINIA E. MAMPRE—HOUSTON, TEXAS

1 box (1 pound) frozen strudel dough, thawed
1½ cups plus 2 tablespoons sweet butter or sweet margarine, melted
¼ cup grated orange rind
1½ teaspoons cinnamon
½ teaspoon nutmeg
3 tablespoons milk or cream
12 ounces semisweet chocolate, melted over simmering
water
1 cup finely chopped almonds, pecans, walnuts, or
pistachios
½ cup coconut flakes

Preheat oven to 375°F.

Cut strudel dough roll into four equal pieces. Work with one piece at a time, keeping the remaining pieces covered with plastic wrap until ready to use.

Unroll ¼ of strudel dough to form a strip with several layers. Cut strip in half through all the layers. Take one cut strip at a time, brush with butter, and place second strip on top. Fold double strips into an accordian shape.

Moisten and pinch together the folds at one end, spreading apart the folds at the opposite end to make a little fan. Place fan on ungreased cookie sheet and brush lightly with butter.

After setting aside 2 tablespoons of the melted butter, repeat process with all the pieces of strudel dough.

Bake at 375°F for 12 to 15 minutes, until golden brown. Set aside to cool.

Mix orange rind, cinnamon, nutmeg, milk, and remaining 2 tablespoons of melted butter into melted chocolate.

Dip wide end of fans into chocolate mixture and then into nuts or coconut or a mixture of both.

Let dipped fans cool and set before storing or serving.

Store in a waxed-paper-lined tin or wrapped in foil.

Yield: approximately 6 dozen fans

CHOCOLATE FANTASY #19

Alchemists working at a secret laboratory hidden within the walls of a monastery high in the Himalaya Mountains of Tibet have announced that they have perfected a process far more valuable than turning base metals into gold. They are now able to transform spinach into chocolate.

Everything a winner should be . . . impressive looking and delicious.

CHOCOLATE PASTRY CAKE

HELEN M. LOWE—LAKE OSWEGO, OREGON

8 ounces chocolate (your choice)
½ cup sugar
½ cup water
1½ teaspoons instant coffee powder
1½ teaspoons vanilla
½ teaspoon almond extract
1 9-ounce or 10-ounce package pie crust mix
2 cups heavy cream
peppermint stick candy

Preheat oven to 425°F.

Combine chocolate, sugar, water, and coffee powder in a saucepan and cook over low heat, stirring constantly, until mixture is smooth. Remove from heat, stir in vanilla and almond extract, and let cool to room temperature.

Blend ¾ cup of the chocolate mixture into the pie crust mix. Divide pie crust into 6 equal portions. Press each portion over the bottom of an inverted 8-inch ungreased round cake pan to within 1 inch of the edge. (Do in relays according to the number of cake pans available.) Bake each portion at 425°F, on a low rack, for about 5 minutes or until done. If necessary, trim layers around edges to make all 6 even.

Let layers cool and then run the tip of a knife under edges to loosen. Lift off carefully. Set aside.

Whip cream until it just begins to hold soft peaks. Fold in the remaining chocolate mixture.

Stack baked pastry layers, spreading chocolate cream between layers and over the top. Chill in refrigerator for at least 8 hours. Trim with peppermint stick candy.

Yield: 10-12 servings

The seashore resort city of Wildwood, New Jersey, held a Chocolate Festival. In addition to the usual chocolate tasting, candy dipping, and fudge making, there were demonstrations of cocoa painting, an art form in which a chef paints a picture on a sugar or almond paste background. The paint is made of cocoa butter and cocoa powders. All the pictures can be eaten.

Rembrandt, Van Gogh, Grandma Moses—eat your hearts out.

Here is absolute proof of the divine connection between the cocoa bean and the human being:

A healthy human being has a temperature of 98.6 degrees Fahrenheit, the same temperature as the melting point of cocoa butter, an essential ingredient in the making of chocolate.

SCRUMPTIOUSLY
CLASSIC

Hollywood, Big Sur, the Golden Gate Bridge and, now, California Apricot Fudge. Every one of them a well-deserved West Coast landmark.

CALIFORNIA APRICOT FUDGE

LIBIA FOGLESONG—SAN BRUNO, CALIFORNIA

3½ cups sugar
1½ cups evaporated milk
dash salt
18 ounces semisweet chocolate
½ cup butter or margarine
⅔ cup chopped dried apricots
1½ cups chopped walnuts
2 tablespoons finely chopped orange peel
2 teaspoons vanilla extract

In a very heavy pot heat sugar, milk, and salt and bring mixture to a boil. Cook over medium-high heat, stirring constantly, for about 7 minutes or until mixture reads soft ball stage on a candy thermometer. Remove from heat.

Combine chocolate, butter, apricots, walnuts, orange peel, and vanilla and pour over hot mixture. Stir until chocolate is melted and mixture is well combined.

Pour into a lightly buttered shallow 9 x 13-inch pan. Let cool.

Cut into tiny squares and, if desired, serve in candy cup papers.

Yield: approximately 7 dozen candies.

In Belgium today, 17,000 people—one out of every 200 workers in the country—are involved in the making, selling, and promotion of chocolate.

Now you know why Belgium is such an important ally of the United States.

CHOCOLATE FANTASY #20

Having the "Hershey Touch," similar to the Midas Touch but without the drawbacks, allowing you—whenever you want—to turn anything you touch into chocolate.

Okay, there is not a lot of chocolate in this cake and it is "only" white chocolate, but for sure you will love this sensational cake.

WHITE CHOCOLATE CAKE

JANICE TORRENCE—WARSAW, INDIANA

> 4 ounces white chocolate
> 1/3 cup boiling water
> 1 cup butter or margarine, softened
> 2 cups sugar
> 4 egg yolks
> 1 teaspoon vanilla
> 2 1/2 cups flour
> 1 teaspoon baking soda
> 1 cup buttermilk
> 4 egg whites, stiffly beaten
> 1 cup pecans
> 1 cup coconut flakes
> Frosting (recipe follows)

Preheat oven to 350°F.

Place chocolate in boiling water and stir until melted. Set aside to cool.

Cream together butter and sugar. Add egg yolks, one at a time, beating well after each addition. Add melted chocolate and vanilla. Sift together flour and baking soda and add to chocolate mixture, alternately with buttermilk. Fold in beaten egg whites. Gently stir in pecans and coconut flakes.

Pour batter into 3 greased and lightly floured 9-inch cake pans.

Bake at 350°F. for 30 minutes or until wooden toothpick tests clean. Let cool and cover with Frosting.

Yield: 10-12 servings

FROSTING

¼ cup butter or margarine, softened
8 ounces cream cheese, softened
2 teaspoons vanilla
3½ cups confectioners' sugar

Combine butter, cream cheese, vanilla, and sugar and beat to spreading consistency.

Montezuma, emperor of the Aztecs in Mexico, was the first chocoholic. Every day he drank 50 cups of chocolate and served 2,000 more to the members of his royal household.

Brownies that are thick and solid like fudge and with the taste of almond . . . magnificent!

ALMOND FUDGE BROWNIES

MURIEL S. FRASER—WATERFORD, CONNECTICUT

4 eggs, separated
6 ounces semisweet chocolate
½ cup butter or margarine, softened
1 cup sugar
3½ ounces, marzipan crumbled into small pieces
1 cup flour
1 teaspoon instant coffee powder dissolved in 2 table-
     spoons hot water
2 teaspoons vanilla
½ cup semisweet chocolate chips
Frosting (recipe follows)

Preheat oven to 350°F.

In a saucepan or double boiler melt the chocolate over boiling water. Remove from heat and set aside.

In a large bowl, beat together butter and sugar until light. Add almond paste, blending well. Add flour, dissolved coffee, melted chocolate, egg yolks, and 1 teaspoon vanilla. Mix together well. In a small bowl, beat egg whites until stiff peaks form. Fold in beaten egg whites. Fold in chocolate chips. Grease and flour the bottom only of a 9 x 13-inch pan. Pour batter into pan and spread evenly.

Bake at 350°F for about 25 minutes, until set. Do not overcook. Remove from oven, let cool, cover with Frosting, and cut into squares.

Yield: approximately 3 dozen brownies

FROSTING

¼ cup sugar
¼ cup packed brown sugar
dash salt
¼ cup milk
2 tablespoons butter or margarine
3 ounces semisweet chocolate
1 cup sifted confectioners' sugar
1 teaspoon vanilla

In a small saucepan, combine sugar, brown sugar, salt, milk, butter, and chocolate. Heat to boiling, stirring constantly.

Remove from heat, stir in confectioners' sugar and vanilla, and beat until smooth.

Louis XIV of France—the Sun King—is remembered for many majestic acts, including building the royal palace at Versailles, being the patron of writers like Molière, and establishing the position of Royal Chocolate Maker to the King.

Although this recipe won handily with vanilla ice cream, feel free to use your own favorite flavor because it is a real winner no matter how you slice it.

 # CHOCOLATE DIABLO DELIGHT

PEG COVERT—WALNUT CREEK, CALIFORNIA

¼ cup butter or margarine, melted
1 cup sugar
¾ cup heavy cream
6 tablespoons unsweetened cocoa powder
¾ cup chopped walnuts
½ gallon vanilla ice cream or ice milk, slightly softened
Crust (recipe follows)

In a medium-sized bowl, combine butter, sugar, heavy cream, and cocoa powder, blending together well. Add chopped nuts.

Cook in a microwave for 1 minute on high or place mixture in a heavy saucepan on med-high heat and stir until melted. Set aside.

Spread ice cream evenly into Crust, filling the entire pie plate. Place in freezer for 10 minutes.

Cut ice cream pie into wedges, reheat chocolate fudge sauce, and pour over each piece. Serve immediately.

Yield: 8-10 servings

12 ounces semisweet chocolate, coarsely chopped
1½ cups crushed walnuts
½ cup flour
½ cup sugar
¼ cup butter or margarine, softened

Preheat oven to 350°F.

Combine chocolate, walnuts, flour, and sugar in a medium bowl. Using a pastry blender or a knife, cut in butter, making a crumb mixture.

Press mixture into a 10-inch pie plate, covering the sides and the bottom of the plate.

Bake at 350°F for 12 to 15 minutes.

Remove from oven and let cool.

Just about everyone likes cheesecake, and this one with a blend of chocolate and peanut butter will surely convert those who do not.

CHOCOLATE PEANUT BUTTER CHEESECAKE

CHARLYNE GOODRICH KNEPPER—PALM BEACH GARDENS, FLORIDA

> 4 ounces semisweet chocolate
> 1½ pounds cream cheese, softened
> 5 eggs
> 1 cup sugar
> ⅔ cup creamy peanut butter
> 1 teaspoon vanilla
> Chocolate Cookie Crust (recipe follows)
> Sour Cream Topping (recipe follows)

Preheat oven to 300°F.

In a saucepan or double boiler melt the chocolate over simmering water. Remove from heat and set aside.

Adding one ingredient at a time, thoroughly mix together cream cheese, eggs, sugar, chocolate, peanut butter, and vanilla.

Pour filling into Chocolate Cookie Crust and bake at 300°F for 40 minutes.

Remove from oven, let cool, and then cover with Sour Cream Topping. Preheat oven to 450°F.

Put cheesecake back in oven and bake at 450°F for 5 minutes. Remove from oven, let cool, and chill in refrigerator.

Yield: 20-24 servings

CHOCOLATE COOKIE CRUST

2 cups chocolate cookie crumbs
1 cup butter or margarine, softened

Mix together well and press into a 9 x 13-inch baking pan.

SOUR CREAM TOPPING

1 pint sour cream
¼ cup sugar
1 teaspoon vanilla

Stir together sour cream, sugar, and vanilla until smooth.

Frozen fudge on a stick, a neat trick . . . it's slick!

CREAMY MOCHA FUDGIE-WUDGIES

IDA DAVIS—DENVER, COLORADO

4 tablespoons cocoa powder
1 tablespoon malted milk powder
½ cup sugar
2 tablespoons cornstarch
1½ cups milk
1 cup cream
½ teaspoon instant coffee powder

Place cocoa powder, malted milk, sugar, and cornstarch in a heavy saucepan. Gradually stir in milk and cream and then cook over low heat, stirring constantly with wire whisk, until mixture becomes thick. Add coffee powder, stirring well.

Remove from heat and let cool slightly.

Pour into popsicle molds and freeze until completely solid.

Yield: 8-10 popsicles

NO WONDER THEY LOST THE EMPIRE

According to a spokesman for the British royal family, Prince Charles does not like chocolate.

CHOCOLATE FANTASY #21

Chocolate toothpaste that prevents cavities and removes plaque.

The raspberry jam gives a very pleasant sweet and tart surprise when you bite through the toasted coconut topping.

CHOCOLATE RASPBERRY BARS

HEATHER FOX—PAWTUCKET, RHODE ISLAND

2 ounces unsweetened chocolate
½ cup butter or margarine
2 eggs
1 cup sugar
1 teaspoon vanilla
1 cup flour
½ teaspoon baking powder
dash salt
½ cup coconut flakes
¼ cup raspberry jam

Preheat oven to 350°F.

Melt chocolate and butter over low heat. Set aside and let cool slightly.

Beat eggs until thick and foamy. Beat in sugar. Stir in chocolate and then add vanilla. Set aside.

Sift together flour, baking powder, and salt. Stir into egg mixture.

Turn into a greased 9-inch square baking pan and bake at 350°F for 25 minutes, until wooden toothpick tests clean. Let cool 15 to 20 minutes in pan on wire rack.

While cake is cooling, spread coconut on an ungreased cookie sheet and place in 350°F oven for about 3 to 5 minutes or until light golden.

Spread raspberry jam over top of cake and sprinkle with toasted coconut. Cut into bars about 2 inches by 3 inches.

Yield: 1 dozen bars

For the Hershey Chocolate Company's 93rd birthday celebration during the Great American Chocolate Festival at the Hotel Hershey in Hershey, Pennsylvania, Albert Kumin, a former White House pastry chef, created a 93-layer chocolate cake that was 9 feet tall.

A perfect not-too-sweet dessert after a South-of-the-Border dinner, a chili cook-off, or a Texas Bar-B-Que.

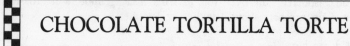

CHOCOLATE TORTILLA TORTE

CLARE DOWDALL—HOUSTON, TEXAS

> 6 ounces semisweet chocolate, coarsely chopped
> 1¼ cups sour cream
> 1 teaspoon cinnamon
> 1 teaspoon vanilla
> 7 6-inch diameter soft flour tortillas
> 1 tablespoon confectioners' sugar
> chocolate shavings
> fresh strawberries (if desired)

In a saucepan or double boiler, combine chocolate, 1 cup of the sour cream, and cinnamon and heat over simmering water, stirring constantly, until chocolate melts and mixture is well blended. Remove from heat and stir in vanilla. Set aside, stirring occasionally, until mixture is firm enough to spread.

Holding a tortilla in your hand, spread the top with approximately 3 tablespoons of the chocolate mixture. Spread to edges, as evenly as possible. Place tortilla on a service plate and repeat the process, placing each covered tortilla on top of the others. Leave the top tortilla unfrosted. Press down on the stack very gently.

Combine the remaining ¼ cup of sour cream with the confectioners' sugar, blending until smooth. Spread over top of the stacked tortillas.

Cover with an inverted bowl that is large enough not to touch the top or sides of the tortilla stack. Refrigerate 8 hours.

Just before serving, garnish with chocolate shavings and, if desired, fresh strawberries.

Cut with a very sharp knife into thin wedges.

Yield: 12-14 servings

REDUCE JOB-RELATED STRESS

Catherine's Chocolates in Great Barrington, Massachusetts, offers revenge for people aggravated at work by their bosses. The company sells a pure milk chocolate bust of an executive—a "corporate head"—complete with pin-striped suit and a tie, so you can chew someone's head off if you want—and enjoy doing it.

The price for this satisfaction: $16.95 postpaid.

CHOCOLATE FANTASY #22

Whenever people feel that the stresses of contemporary life have become excessive and overwhelming, they can go to a chocotorium for rest, recuperation, and rejuvenation.

"WAR IS HELL" DEPARTMENT

Three hundred British war brides, representing the 70,000 British women who married American servicemen stationed in the United Kingdom during World War II, held a 40-year reunion in Southampton, England, in September, 1986.

Some of the women brought with them the war-era gifts they received from their husbands, including nylon stockings and, of course, chocolate.

An easier version but just as delicious as that old-time favorite.

CHOCOLATE TURTLES

MILDRED FAVINGER—AKRON, OHIO

12 ounces caramels
2 tablespoons milk
¼ teaspoon vanilla
2 cups pecans
1 ounce milk chocolate
2 ounces semisweet chocolate

In a saucepan or double boiler combine caramels and milk and melt over boiling water. Add vanilla and pecans, stirring until thoroughly mixed.

Remove from heat and drop by teaspoonfuls onto a greased cookie sheet.

Let candies cool. In a saucepan or double boiler, melt the chocolates over simmering water. Remove from heat. Dip cooled candies into chocolate. Let cool again.

Yield: approximately 3 dozen candies

What is a chocolate fantasy without a hot fudge sauce to pour over absolutely everything?

HOT FUDGE SAUCE

PATRICIA GOOCH—BROCKTON, MASSACHUSETTS

> 2 ounces unsweetened chocolate
> ½ cup butter or margarine
> 2 cups sifted confectioners' sugar
> ¾ cup evaporated milk
> 1 to 2 teaspoons chocolate liqueur

In a saucepan or double boiler melt chocolate and butter over simmering water. Remove from heat and add, alternately, sugar and evaporated milk.

Return sauce to heat and simmer for 8 to 10 minutes, stirring constantly. Mix in chocolate liqueur.

Yield: approximately 2 cups sauce

What more could a host or hostess want: a great cake that makes a lasting impression and is easy to make.

SCRUMPTIOUS CHOCOLATE
MOUSSE REFRIGERATOR CAKE

ROSE BETAR—OCEAN, NEW JERSEY

2 tablespoons sugar
4 tablespoons water
12 ounces chocolate (your choice)
6 eggs, separated
1 teaspoon vanilla
1 cup heavy cream, whipped
plain ladyfingers
whipped cream
shaved chocolate

Place sugar, water, and chocolate in a saucepan or double boiler and melt over simmering water. Remove from heat.

Beat the egg yolks and add them, a little at a time, to the chocolate mixture. Add vanilla. Beat egg whites until stiff and fold in. Fold in whipped cream.

Place ladyfingers around the sides and then the bottom of a greased 9-inch springform pan. Pour half the batter into the pan. Arrange a layer of ladyfingers over top of batter and pour remaining batter over ladyfingers.

Refrigerate cake for 24 hours.

Just before serving, garnish with whipped cream and shaved chocolate.

Yield: 10-12 servings

WHEN YOU CARE ENOUGH TO THANK THE VERY BEST

For $12.95, de Geneve Chocolatier of Madison, Wisconsin, has a way for you to show your appreciation so other people really know you mean it.

The company makes a "Thank You Medallion," packed in a beautiful decorator box, that has "thank you" written in four languages—English, Spanish, French, and German—around the edges of an 8½-inch, 12-ounce floral medallion made of pure milk chocolate.

CHOCOLATE FANTASY #23

First there was oil-based paint, then water-based paint, and now, best of all, chocolate-based paint.

INDESCRIBABLY
SINFUL

Yogurt is not usually found in cheesecake, and it gives this one a pleasantly tangy taste.

TANGY CHOCOLATE CHEESECAKE

MARY B. WOLFE—GLENDALE, ARIZONA

3 ounces sweet chocolate
3 ounces semisweet chocolate
2 tablespoons flour
½ cup sugar
¼ teaspoon salt
1 pound cream cheese, softened
½ teaspoon vanilla
1 teaspoon lemon juice
2 large eggs, separated
½ cup plain yogurt
Chocolate German Cracker Crust (recipe follows)

Preheat oven to 300°F.

In a saucepan or double boiler melt the chocolates over simmering water. Remove from heat to cool.

Into a small bowl, sift together flour, sugar, and salt. Set aside.

In a medium mixing bowl, blend together at medium speed the cream cheese, vanilla, and lemon juice. Add melted chocolates and then the flour mixture, mixing well. Continue to mix on medium speed, add egg yolks and yogurt, blending until creamy. Set aside.

Using clean beaters and a small bowl, beat egg whites until soft peaks form. Fold egg whites into cream cheese mixture.

Pour filling into cooled Chocolate Graham Cracker Crust and bake at 300°F for 45 to 55 minutes or until an inserted knife comes out clean.

Chill completely in refrigerator before serving.

Yield: 6-8 servings

CHOCOLATE GRAHAM CRACKER CRUST

3 ounces semisweet chocolate
1½ cups graham cracker crumbs
6 tablespoons butter or margarine, softened

Preheat oven to 375°F.

In a saucepan or double boiler melt the chocolate over simmering water. Remove from heat to cool.

Mix together melted chocolate, graham cracker crumbs, and butter.

Firmly press crust mixture into a 9-inch pie pan and bake at 375°F for 5 to 6 minutes.

Remove from oven and let cool.

Theobroma caca, the scientific name for chocolate, comes from the Greek words meaning "cacoa, the food of the gods."
Does that make chocolate the ultimate ethnic food?

This candy is an archaeologist's dream: layers of delight to dig through for delicious discoveries. First a layer of semi-sweet and unsweetened chocolates; then a layer of marshmallow creme followed by a crunchy layer of peanut butter and graham cracker crumbs; and, finally, a layer of milk chocolate. A treasure to rival King Tut's tomb!

■ CHOCOLATE COMBINATION TREAT ■

FRAN VIGIL—ALBUQUERQUE, NEW MEXICO

> 12 ounces milk chocolate
> 1 cup butter or margarine, melted
> 1½ cups graham cracker crumbs
> ½ cup chunky peanut butter
> 2 cups confectioners' sugar
> 1 cup marshmallow creme
> 12 ounces semisweet chocolate
> 2 ounces unsweetened chocolate

In a saucepan or double boiler melt the milk chocolate over simmering water. Remove from heat and spread evenly in the bottom of a lightly greased 9 x 13-inch pan. Place in freezer until hard.

Combine butter, graham cracker crumbs, peanut butter, and sugar. Mix together well. Press on top of layer of hard milk chocolate in pan. Using a knife that is repeatedly dipped in hot water, evenly spread marshmallow creme over graham cracker crumb mixture.

In saucepan or double boiler melt the dark chocolates over simmering water, remove from heat, and pour over marshmallow creme layer in pan. Spread chocolate evenly to edges of pan, covering the marshmallow creme.

Place in refrigerator until chocolate is completely hard.

Cut into squares.

Yield: approximately 5 dozen squares

CHOCOLATE FANTASY #24

The close passage to earth by an errant comet has caused all the snow everywhere to turn into chocolate . . . and you have just been transferred to Alaska.

What better "fruit of your labors" could there be than these peaches in chocolate sauce, a top choice when a sophisticated dessert is desired.

PEACHES 'N' CHOCOLATE CREME

CYNTHIA GOLDEN—ATLANTA, GEORGIA

1 cup orange juice
1 cup apple juice
½ cup sugar
1 whole clove
1 cinnamon stick
4 peaches or nectarines, peeled and sliced
1 quart peach ice cream or ice milk
Chocolate Mint Sauce (recipe follows)

Mix together orange juice, apple juice, and sugar in a heavy saucepan. Add clove and cinnamon stick and heat to boiling over moderate heat, stirring constantly. Let boil for 3 minutes, reduce heat, and add peaches. Simmer for 5 to 6 minutes.

Remove from heat and set aside.

Put ice cream into individual serving dishes. Remove peaches from syrup with a slotted spoon and place over ice cream. Spoon chocolate Mint Sauce over peaches.

Yield: 4 servings

CHOCOLATE MINT SAUCE

2 ounces unsweetened chocolate
2 ounces semisweet chocolate
¼ cup light corn syrup
½ cup heavy cream
3 tablespoons chocolate mint liqueur

Combine chocolates, corn syrup, and heavy cream in a saucepan or double boiler and heat over simmering water until the mixture is melted and smooth.

Remove from heat and add chocolate mint liqueur, stirring well.

According to Casanova, the legendary Italian lover and adventurer, chocolate was more effective than champagne for encouraging romance.

CHOCOLATE FANTASY #25

Chocolate telephones for something to nibble on when you are put on hold.

Two workers in Switzerland were arrested in 1980 for trying to sell state secrets to the Soviet Union and China. The secrets they were offering included 40 recipes for making chocolate.
You can't trust anyone these days.

The image of velvet is deep, dark, luxurious, and rich . . . exactly the right words to describe this masterpiece.

CHOCOLATE VELVET

JUDY SMITLEY—HARRISBURG, PENNSYLVANIA

12 ounces sweet chocolate
4 ounces milk chocolate
6 tablespoons butter or margarine
½ cup confectioners' sugar
3 egg yolks
1 teaspoon vanilla
2 tablespoons crème de cacao
½ teaspoon instant coffee powder
2 cups heavy cream, whipped stiff
3 egg whites, beaten until soft peaks form
whipped cream (if desired)

In a saucepan or double boiler melt chocolates and butter over simmering water. Remove from heat and set aside.

Mix together sugar, egg yolks, vanilla, crème de cacao, and coffee powder. Stir in melted chocolate and butter. Fold in whipped cream, blending thoroughly. Fold in egg whites.

Turn mixture into a 10-inch springform pan. (To fill pan completely, this recipe must be doubled.) Refrigerate overnight. Unmold on a chilled plate. Garnish with whipped cream, if desired.

Yield: 8-10 servings

There is no chance that this cake can be accused of false advertising . . . it really is fantastic . . . and will become an immediate family favorite.

FANTASTIC CHOCOLATE LAYER CAKE

MRS. VICTOR TRAGER—WOODHAVEN, NEW YORK

4 ounces unsweetened chocolate
½ cup butter or margarine
2 cups sugar
½ teaspoon vanilla
¼ teaspoon salt
2 eggs
¼ pint sour cream mixed with 1½ teaspoons baking soda
2 cups flour
1 cup boiling water
1 tablespoon cognac or rum
8 ounces apricot preserves
Icing (recipe follows)

Preheat oven to 350°F.

Place chocolate and butter in a small saucepan and heat, stirring, over low heat until mixture is melted and smooth.

Transfer to large bowl and add sugar, vanilla, and salt, beating just enough to mix. Add eggs, one at a time, beating after each additon. Beat in sour cream and baking soda. Slowly beat in flour just until mixture is blended and smooth. Very gradually add water, beating just until smooth. Add cognac. Mixture will be thin.

Greast two 9-inch cake pans, line the bottoms with waxed paper, and then grease and flour the waxed paper. Divide batter into two equal portions and pour into the two prepared cake pans.

Bake at 350° F for 25 minutes or until a wooden toothpick tests clean. Remove from oven and cool in pans on racks for 10 minutes. Loosen edges and invert on racks. Remove waxed paper and let cool completely.

Place one layer upside down on a platter and cover top with apricot preserves. Place other layer right side up on top of first layer and spread icing over top and sides.

Yield: 10-12 servings

ICING

> 2 *ounces unsweetened chocolate*
> 2 *tablespoons unsalted butter or unsalted margarine*
> 1 *cup confectioners' sugar*
> 2 *tablespoons boiling water*

Heat chocolate and butter in a saucepan over low heat, stirring constantly, until melted and smooth.

Remove from heat and beat in sugar until smooth. Work in water, stir until smooth.

Spread on cake immediately.

More chocolate is made in the United States than in any other country.

Is this a great country, or what?

(And more chocolate is made in Pennsylvania than in any other state.)

In 1939, Nestlé became the first company to sell ready-made chocolate chips. Today, Nestlé produces nearly 140 million each day, or 50 billion a year.

Hershey makes about 20 million kisses daily, over 7 billion each year.

Tempt-Me Truffles . . . and indeed they will.

TEMPT-ME TRUFFLES

WANDA PINKSTON—DIGHTON, KANSAS

> 5 ounces unsweetened chocolate
> 8 ounces cream cheese, softened
> 4 cups confectioners' sugar
> 1 teaspoon vanilla
> ½ cup chopped almonds
> cocoa powder
> confectioners' sugar

In a saucepan or double boiler melt the chocolate over simmering water. Remove from heat.

Place cream cheese in a large mixing bowl and gradually add confectioners' sugar, mixing well after each addition. Add chocolate and vanilla, mixing together well.

Place in refrigerator to chill for several hours.

Preheat oven to 350°F.

Place almonds on an ungreased cookie sheet and bake at 350°F for 4 to 5 minutes.

Shape candy into 1-inch balls. Roll some of the candy in toasted almonds, some in cocoa powder, and some in confectioners' sugar. Chill in refrigerator before serving.

Store in refrigerator.

Yield: approximately 4 dozen truffles

What could be more luscious than a cheesecake? A cheesecake loaded with macadamia nuts . . . and chocolate.

MACADAMIA MOCHA CHEESECAKE

RUTH SNIDER—IOWA CITY, IOWA

1½ cups chocolate cookie crumbs
1 cup finely ground macadamia nuts
½ teaspoon cinnamon
¾ cup butter or margarine, melted
1 cup sugar
3 eggs
1½ pounds cream cheese, softened
8 ounces semisweet chocolate, melted
1 teaspoon instant coffee powder dissolved in 1 teaspoon
   of water
2 tablespoons cocoa powder
1 teaspoon vanilla extract
3 cups sour cream
¾ cup chopped macadamia nuts
1 cup heavy cream, whipped
chocolate curls
½ cup whole macadamia nuts

In a small bowl, mix together cookie crumbs, ground macadamia nuts, and cinnamon. Blend in ½ cup melted butter and pour mixture into the

■ 108 ■

center of a well-buttered 9-inch springform pan. Flatten mixture over bottom of pan and press along sides. Chill shell in refrigerator.

Preheat oven to 350°F.

In a medium bowl, beat sugar and eggs until the mixture is light and then stir in cream cheese. Stir in melted chocolate, dissolved coffee, cocoa powder, and vanilla extract, mixing thoroughly. Beat in sour cream and chopped macadamia nuts. Fold in remaining ¼ cup melted butter.

Pour batter into chilled shell.

Bake at 350°F for 45 minutes. Remove from oven, let cool slightly, and then chill in refrigerator. Cake may seem quite liquid but it will become firm when chilled.

Just before serving, decorate with whipped cream, chocolate curls, and whole macadamia nuts.

Yield: 10-12 servings

Americans eat an average of about 12 pounds of chocolate per person each year. This ranks the United States number five among the countries of the world.

The most chocolate consumed per capita—22 pounds per year per person—is in Switzerland, followed by England (15.4 pounds), West Germany (13.8 pounds), Belgium (13.6 pounds), the United States (12 pounds), and Sweden and Austria tied at 11.6 pounds each.

CHOCOLATE FANTASY #26

A transcontinental pipeline with branches leading into every community in the United States has just been completed, assuring uninterrupted supplies of chocolate to Americans everywhere.

Because chocolate melts so readily, it used to be replaced during the hot summer months by other candies, especially caramels. Now, thanks to better packaging and transportation, refrigeration, and air conditioning, chocolate can be enjoyed all year round.

Progress marches onward!

A cold, windy, snowy night; a roaring fireplace; and a hot cup of special chocolate cocoa . . . ahhh!

CHOCOLATE LUSTRE

JAN E. SHELTON—ESCONDIDO, CALIFORNIA

⅔ cup unsweetened cocoa powder
1 cup sugar
dash salt
⅔ cup hot water
½ cup creamy peanut butter
6 cups half-and-half or milk
2 to 4 tablespoons orange liqueur or coffee liqueur, to
    taste

Combine cocoa powder, sugar, and salt in a large suacepan. Blend in water.

Cook, stirring constantly, until mixture comes to a boil. Let boil for 2 minutes.

Remove from heat and add peanut butter, stirring until smooth. Mix in half-and-half and heat through, but do not boil. Mix thoroughly.

Remove from heat and stir in liqueur. Serve hot in mugs.

Yield: 8 servings

A tart by any other name would not be as good because it would not have the three essential ingredients—white chocolate, dark chocolate, and raspberries—that made this one a sure winner.

WHITE AND DARK CHOCOLATE RASPBERRY TART

LENORE ERICKSON—ROCKFORD, ILLINOIS

1 unbaked pie crust
1 10-ounce package frozen raspberries
1 tablespoon cornstarch
1 tablespoon sugar
1 cup raspberries (if available, use fresh)
4 ounces white chocolate
½ cup plus 2 tablespoons butter or margarine, softened
⅓ cup sugar
2 eggs
2 ounces semisweet chocolate
chocolate leaves
raspberries (if available, use fresh)

Preheat oven to 450°F.

Place pie crust into an ungreased 10-inch tart or springform pan. Press crust up sides 1 inch and prick crust.

Bake at 450°F for 9 to 11 minutes, until browned. Set aside.

Puree frozen raspberries in a blender or food processor. Strain and discard seeds. Combine cornstarch and sugar in a small saucepan. Gradually add raspberry puree. Cook over low heat, stirring constantly, until mixture thickens.

Remove from heat and let cool. Spread over baked pie crust and top with fresh raspberries. Set aside to chill in refrigerator.

In a saucepan or double boiler melt white chocolate over simmering water. Remove from heat.

In a small bowl beat ½ cup softened butter and sugar until light and fluffy. Gradually add melted white chocolate, beating constantly. Add eggs, 1 at a time, beating at highest speed for 3 minutes after adding each egg. Pour over raspberry mixture. Refrigerate until set.

In a small saucepan melt semisweet chocolate and remaining 2 tablespoons butter. Carefully pour over white chocolate layer.

Refrigerate for at least 2 hours. Remove from refrigerator and let stand before serving about 30 minutes to soften chocolate layers.

Garnish with chocolate leaves and raspberries.

Yield: 10-12 servings

CHOCOLATE FANTASY #27

Sleep researchers have discovered that placing a single chocolate chip under one's tongue just before drifting off to sleep will produce at least eight hours of dreams about chocolate.

Hepburn and Tracy and cheesecake and brownies . . . two of the great pairings of the 20th century.

CHEESECAKE BROWNIES

JOANNA MOORE—PAULS VALLEY, OKLAHOMA

½ cup butter or margarine, softened
8 ounces cream cheese, softened
1½ cups sugar
3 eggs
1 teaspoon instant coffee powder
1½ teaspoons hot water
¾ cup flour
½ cup unsweetened cocoa powder
½ teaspoon salt
1½ teaspoons vanilla
1 cup chopped pecans

Preheat oven to 350°F.

Cream butter and cream cheese. Add sugar, beating well. Beat in, one at a time, eggs, coffee powder, hot water, flour, cocoa powder, salt, vanilla, and chopped pecans.

Pour batter into a greased 9-inch square pan and bake at 350°F for about 30 minutes, until wooden toothpick tests clean.

Cut into 2-inch squares.

Yield: 16 brownies

What is simple to make but impossible to stop eating? Chocolate Meringue Pie, of course!

CHOCOLATE MERINGUE PIE

LILLIAN F. OGLE—RICHMOND, VIRGINIA

½ cup unsweetened cocoa powder or 3 ounces unsweetened chocolate
2½ cups milk
1½ cups plus 6 tablespoons sugar
2 tablespoons flour
½ teaspoon salt
3 eggs, separated
2 tablespoons butter or margarine
2 teaspoons vanilla
1 9-inch pie crust of your choice

Place cocoa powder or chocolate, milk, 1½ cups of the sugar, flour, salt, egg yolks, butter, and vanilla in a saucepan and heat, with stirring, to boiling. Continue heating, with stirring, until mixture becomes thick.

Remove from heat and pour filling into pie crust. Set aside.

Beat egg whites and then mix in remaining 6 tablespoons of sugar. Spoon over top of filling and place under broiler for 2 to 3 minutes or until golden brown.

Yield: 8-10 servings

Although the great Spanish explorer Hernando Cortez brought the first chocolate back to Europe in 1528, until 1847 it was consumed only as a drink. It took over three hundred years for manufacturing processes to be developed that could convert cocoa powder into solid chocolate bars for eating.

DECADENTLY
STUPENDOUS

Betty Grable's cheesecake and Stanley Haden's cheesecake . . . both worthy of note.

TRIPLE CHOCOLATE CHEESECAKE

STANLEY H. HADEN—BIRMINGHAM, ALABAMA

> 2 ounces unsweetened chocolate
> 2 ounces white chocolate
> 2 ounces semisweet chocolate
> 3 eggs
> ¾ cup sugar
> 1½ pounds cream cheese, softened
> 2 teaspoons vanilla
> 1 ounce white rum
> Crust (recipe follows)

Preheat oven to 250°F.

In a saucepan or double boiler, one at a time, melt the three chocolates over simmering water. Remove from heat, keeping each separate, and set aside.

Place eggs and sugar in a bowl and mix until frothy. Add cream cheese, ⅓ at a time, beating until smooth. Add 1 teaspoon of the vanilla and mix for 1 minute. Divide mixture into three equal portions.

Combine unsweetened chocolate, ½ ounce of the rum, and ⅓ of the cheesecake batter and stir together well. Pour into Crust, spreading evenly over bottom.

Combine white chocolate and ⅓ of the cheesecake batter, mixing together well. Very slowly pour over unsweetened chocolate layer.

Combine semisweet chocolate, remaining ½ ounce of the rum, remaining 1 teaspoon of vanilla, and remaining ⅓ of the cheesecake batter. Very slowly pour on top of white chocolate layer.

Bake at 250°F for about 1½ hours, until firm to the touch. Remove from oven and let cool for 1 hour. Chill in refrigerator for at least 12 hours. Slice with a hot knife.

Yield: 12-14 servings

CRUST

1¼ cups graham cracker crumbs
2½ tablespoons butter or margarine, melted
¼ cup sugar

Preheat oven to 350°F.

Combine graham cracker crumbs, butter, and sugar and press into a buttered 9-inch springform pan, covering the sides and bottom.

Bake at 350°F for 10 minutes. Remove from oven and let cool.

Food scientists have tried for years—without any success at all—to make synthetic chocolate. The task may well be impossible because chocolate contains hundreds of different substances and research has not yet uncovered which ingredients or combination of ingredients are responsible for the distinctive flavor.

Chocolate fantasy—chocolate fondue. For many chocolate lovers these two mean the same thing.

CHOCOLATE PLUS FONDUE

THELMA ROSS—LAS VEGAS, NEVADA

1 tablespoon sweet butter or sweet margarine
2 cups sugar
1½ cups evaporated milk
2 ounces bitter chocolate
10 ounces semisweet chocolate
¼ cup marshmallow creme
1 to 2 tablespoons rum
mandarin orange slices, banana slices, apple wedges,
pineapple chunks, pound cake cubes, angel food cake
pieces, large marshmallows, and/or hulled strawberries

Combine butter, sugar, and ¾ cup of the evaporated milk in a saucepan and cook over low heat, stirring constantly, until mixture boils. Simmer for 5 minutes.

Add remaining ¾ cup of the evaporated milk and chocolates. Stir until chocolate has melted and mixture is smooth.

Remove from heat and stir in marshmallow creme and rum.

Pour into fondue pot and serve immediately.

Dip mandarin orange slices, banana slices, apple wedges, pineapple chunks, pound cake cubes, angel food cake pieces, marshmallows, and/or strawberries into fondue.

Yield: 6-8 servings

"Bloom," although nice when associated with flowers, is not too nice in connection with chocolate. Bloom is the whitish film that forms on chocolate when the chocolate has been temporarily exposed to heat or sunlight, causing the cocoa butter to melt a little, and then harden when it returns to room temperature. Bloom looks bad, ruining the characteristic glossiness of chocolate, but it does not spoil the flavor or the quality.

To avoid bloom, keep chocolate in a cool, dry place away from moisture, heat, and direct sunlight.

If you must refrigerate or freeze chocolate, keep it wrapped it in its original container or tightly sealed in plastic to protect it from absorbing the odors of other foods. Chocolate can be stored in the freezer but it is usually not necessary. Chocolate keeps well, at least a year for dark chocolate, six months or more for milk chocolate. Cocoa butter does not go rancid as other fats do.

CHOCOLATE FANTASY #28

A portable intravenous device that provides a constant unobtrusive infusion of chocolate during business meetings, awards ceremonies, and presidential news conferences.

This chocolate-strawberry mousse with chocolate-dipped strawberries is a most sophisticated dessert that would be very much at home at any elegant dinner party.

CHOCOLATE-STRAWBERRY OPULENCE A LA CREME

LISA ARLEDGE—HOUSTON, TEXAS

1 10-ounce package frozen strawberries, thawed but not drained
2 tablespoons superfine sugar
2 ounces semisweet chocolate
8 ounces cream cheese, softened
1/4 cup sour cream
2/3 cup confectioners' sugar
1 teaspoon vanilla
1 cup heavy cream
Chocolate Dipped Strawberries (recipe follows)

Puree strawberries in blender. Press through a fine strainer to extract as much juice as possible. Discard whatever pulp remains in strainer. Measure out 1/4 cup of the juice from the strained strawberries and mix with the superfine sugar. Set aside separately the strained juice mixed with sugar and the remaining strawberry juice.

In a saucepan or double boiler melt the chocolate over simmering water. Remove from heat.

Beat cream cheese and sour cream using an electric mixer until light and fluffy. Mix in confectioners' sugar, vanilla, and melted chocolate. In a separate bowl, whip heavy cream into soft peaks and gently fold into cream cheese mixture.

Line a 6-cup mold with dampened cheesecloth, extending it over the edges. First pour in the ¼ cup of strawberry juice and sugar mixture and then gently spoon in the cream cheese mixture. Spread the cream cheese mixture evenly in the mold. Cover with the cheesecloth that was hanging over the edges.

Chill in refrigerator for 8 hours or overnight.

Just before serving, pull back cheesecloth and invert onto a platter. Carefully remove all the cheesecloth. Garnish with Chocolate Dipped Strawberries and serve the reserved strained strawberry juice as a topping.

Yield: 6-8 servings

CHOCOLATE DIPPED STRAWBERRIES

8 ounces semisweet chocolate
12 to 16 strawberries, washed, dried, and at room temperature

In a saucepan or double boiler melt the chocolate over simmering water. Remove from heat and stir smooth.

Dip each strawberry ⅔ deep in the melted chocolate. Shake gently to remove excess chocolate.

Place dipped strawberries on a cookie sheet covered with waxed paper. Refrigerate about 30 minutes, until chocolate is set. Serve at room temperature.

BECOME A GENUINE CONNOISSEUR

How can you recognize good chocolate?

According to Chocosuisse, the trade association of Swiss chocolate companies, the following are characteristics to look for:

- an unblemished, silky sheen
- when you break off a piece, it breaks firmly and crispy, the edges are clean and the surfaces of the break do not crumble away
- the aroma is full and rounded without being obtrusive and it smells of chocolate and not cocoa
- in your mouth, it melts like butter, does not cling stickily to the palate, feel gritty on the tongue, or leave any aftertaste
- the flavor is fine, delicate, and unique.

Decision time again—do you use creamy or chunky peanut butter for this pie? The answer: one is just as great as the other.

PEANUT BUTTER PIE

JACKIE JIMESON—MARION, NORTH CAROLINA

8 ounces cream cheese, softened
1 cup confectioners' sugar
¾ cup peanut butter
½ cup milk
8 ounces frozen whipped topping, thawed
1 cup miniature chocolate chips
2 9-inch graham cracker crust pie shells
3 ounces chocolate
1 teaspoon solid shortening

Cream together cream cheese, sugar, and peanut butter. Stir in milk and fold in whipped topping. Stir in chocolate chips.

Pour filling into pie shells.

Melt together chocolate and shortening and then spread over tops of pies.

Place pies in freezer for 6 to 8 hours, until firm.

Yield: 16-20 servings

If you have been searching for a delectable combination of crunchy, creamy, and gooey almond-flavored chocolate, you have found it right here.

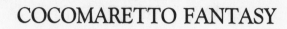

COCOMARETTO FANTASY

NANCY J. BENNETT—SOUTH LAKE TAHOE, CALIFORNIA

½ cup toasted almonds, chopped
3 egg whites
¼ teaspoon cream of tartar
1 cup sugar
2 tablespoons unsweetened cocoa powder, sifted
Mousse Filling (recipe follows)
Fudge Topping (recipe follows)
maraschino cherries with stems

Preheat oven to 375°F.

Spread chopped almonds on an ungreased cookie sheet and place in a 375° F oven for about 5 to 8 minutes, until brown. Set aside.

Reduce oven to 275°F.

Beat egg whites and cream of tartar until stiff peaks form. Gradually add sugar and beat until mixture becomes thick and shiny and holds stiff peaks. Beat in cocoa powder. Fold in toasted almonds.

Spoon batter into a 9-inch round on a cookie sheet that has been covered with brown paper, or form into 8 individual shells. Use the back of a wet spoon to form sides ½ to 1-inch high around the shells.

Bake at 275°F for 1 hour. Turn off heat and let cool in oven.

Spoon Mouse Filling on top of meringue round or into meringue shells. Chill in refrigerator for 1 hour.

Just before serving, pour Fudge Topping over the Mousse Filling. Garnish with maraschino cherries.

MOUSSE FILLING

3 cups heavy cream
1½ cups confectioners' sugar, sifted
¼ cup unsweetened cocoa powder, sifted
dash salt
2 tablespoons amaretto liqueur

Chill beaters and a large bowl in the refrigerator. Beat together cream, sugar, cocoa powder, salt, and amaretto liqueur until soft peaks form.

Yield: 8-10 servings

A 4,484-pound, 10-foot high, chocolate Easter Egg was made in Melbourne, Australia.

6 tablespoons unsweetened cocoa powder, sifted
1 cup sugar
2/3 cup evaporated milk
1/4 cup butter or margarine
1/4 teaspoon salt
1 tablespoon amaretto liqueur
1 teaspoon vanilla

Mix together cocoa and sugar. Add milk.

Bring to a rolling boil over medium-low heat, stirring constantly. Boil, while stirring, for 1 minute more. Add butter, stirring until melted. Add salt, amaretto liqueur, and vanilla.

Remove from heat and let cool to lukewarm.

Yield: 8-10 servings

SHOW THIS TO YOUR MOTHER

According to the American Dental Association, researchers at the Massachusetts Institute of Technology, the Forsyth Dental Center, and other research centers, have discovered that chocolate actually helps reduce cavities in three different ways:

1. Chocolate in the mouth blocks a bacterial enzyme that converts sucrose into a sticky form of sugar that leads to plaque build-up and cavities.
2. Plain milk chocolate reacts with fluoride in saliva to replace lost calcium.
3. The cocoa butter in plain milk chocolate melts quickly, acting as an agent to carry food particles away from the teeth, thereby minimizing contact with teeth.

Napoleon Bonaparte carried chocolate with him whenever he went off to battle and would pop some into his mouth whenever he wanted quick energy.

This cake combines the delicious flavors of almond pralines and raspberries topped with a roof of thick, rich, shingle-like pieces of chocolate.

CHOCOLATE RASPBERRY CAKE

JENNIFER OBUE—MANCHESTER, CONNECTICUT

Almond Pralines (recipe follows)
6 ounces semisweet chocolate
4 egg whites
1¼ cups sugar
3 egg yolks
1 egg
½ cup flour
½ cup cocoa powder
2½ tablespoons butter or margarine, melted and cooled
½ cup water
¼ cup raspberry liqueur
2 cups heavy cream
1 pound semisweet chocolate, grated
⅓ cup raspberry preserves

Preheat oven to 350°F.

Prepare Almond Pralines.

In a saucepan or double boiler melt chocolate over simmering water.

Pour melted chocolate onto a greased cookie sheet covered with waxed paper, and spread evenly, about ⅛-inch thick. Place sheet of chocolate in freezer until firm.

Beat egg yolks, whole egg, ½ cup of sugar, and ½ cup pulverized Almond Pralines until mixture becomes thick and lemon colored. Sift flour and cocoa powder and add to mixture. Beat egg whites until foamy and gradually add ¼ cup of the sugar, continuing to beat until stiff peaks form. Set aside. Gently fold in egg whites by thirds. Stir in melted butter.

Place a piece of waxed paper on the bottom of a greased loaf pan (9x5x3) and pour batter into pan. Bake at 350°F for about 40 minutes, until wooden toothpick tests clean.

Let cool slightly and remove cake from pan. Place cake on a wire rack and set aside.

Mix water and remaining ½ cup sugar together over high heat until sugar dissolves. Bring to boil and let boil for 1 minute. Remove from heat, let cool, and then stir in raspberry liqueur. Set this raspberry syrup aside.

Place heavy cream in a saucepan, heat to boiling, remove from heat, and add grated chocolate. Stir well until chocolate has melted and mixture is smooth.

Put pan in a bowl of ice water and beat until chocolate mixture has the consistency of whipped cream. Transfer chocolate from pan to a bowl to prevent mixture from becoming too firm. Set chocolate cream aside.

Cut cake into three layers. Brush the top of each layer with ⅓ of the raspberry syrup. On two of the layers, spread raspberry preserves over the raspberry syrup. Spread about half of the chocolate cream over top of raspberry preserves, saving the other half of the chocolate cream for frosting cake.

Place one of the cake layers with chocolate cream on top of the other layer with chocolate cream. Place the remaining cake layer on top of the stacked layers, syrup side down.

Frost entire cake with remaining chocolate cream. Break sheet of chocolate into different-sized shinglelike pieces and place on top and sides of cake. Cake should have a rustic appearance.

Sprinkle top with remaining Almond Pralines, making diagonal lines. Store in refrigerator and remove about 1 hour before serving.

Yield: 12-14 servings

ALMOND PRALINES

½ cup slivered almonds
½ cup sugar
2 tablespoons water
⅛ teaspoon cream of tartar

Preheat oven to 350°F.

Place almonds on an ungreased cookie sheet and bake at 350°F for 4 to 5 minutes. Set aside.

Put sugar, water, and cream of tartar in a heavy saucepan and bring to a boil, stirring occasionally. Continue stirring until mixture is bubbly and begins to turn a deep amber color.

Remove from heat, quickly stir in toasted almonds, and pour onto a cookie sheet. Place in freezer until cool. When cool, break up and pulverize in a food processor or blender. Set aside in refrigerator.

These delicate and lacy cookies will disappear as quickly as snowflakes in the middle of July.

REALLY GOOD CHEW-Y CHOCOLATE-Y COOKIES

AMY WOLF—ST. PAUL, MINNESOTA

1/2 cup butter or margarine
1 1/2 cups brown sugar
12 ounces chocolate (your choice)
2 eggs
2 teaspoons vanilla
1/2 cup chopped nuts

Preheat oven to 375°F.

Combine butter and brown sugar in a heavy saucepan and bring to a boil. Boil for 3 minutes, stirring constantly. Stir in chocolate.

Remove from heat and let cool for 5 minutes. Add eggs, 1 at a time, mixing after each addition. Add vanilla and nuts.

Drop batter by half-teaspoonfuls 4 inches apart onto a cookie sheet covered with aluminum foil. Change foil after every other batch.

Bake at 375°F for about 10 minutes. Let cool and then carefully remove cookies from foil.

Yield: approximately 8 dozen cookies

There are few things as good as the taste of fresh oranges and chocolate together in a rich creamy cheesecake.

THE ULTIMATE CHOCOLATE SWIRL CHEESECAKE

DIANE MILLER—STATEN ISLAND, NEW YORK

> Crust (recipe follows)
> 2½ pounds cream cheese
> 1¾ cups sugar
> 2 teaspoons grated orange peel
> ¼ teaspoon vanilla
> 5 eggs
> 2 egg yolks
> ¼ cup heavy cream
> 3 tablespoons flour
> 12 ounces semisweet chocolate
> ½ cup heavy cream, whipped
> chocolate curls (if desired)

Prepare Crust.

Preheat oven to 500°F.

In a large mixing bowl, blend at high speed cream cheese, sugar, orange peel, and vanilla. Beat in eggs and then egg yolks one at a time. Beat in heavy cream and flour, occasionally scraping sides of bowl with spatula, until smooth. Divide mixture in half.

In a saucepan or double boiler melt the chocolate over simmering water.

Stir melted chocolate into one half of the filling. Pour into Crust. Gently pour other half of batter (without the chocolate) over top and swirl chocolate batter through plain batter to marbleize.

Bake at 500°F for 10 minutes and then reduce heat to 250°F and bake for 1 hour more.

Remove from oven and let cool for 2 hours. Then refrigerate for 3 hours or overnight until well chilled.

To serve, loosen crust from sides of pan with spatula and remove sides of pan. Garnish with whipped cream and, if desired, chocolate curls.

CRUST

> 1 cup sifted flour
> ¼ cup sugar
> 1 teaspoon grated lemon peel
> ¼ teaspoon vanilla
> ¼ teaspoon chocolate liqueur or Kahlua
> 1 egg yolk
> ¼ cup butter or margarine, softened

Preheat oven to 400°F.

In a medium-sized bowl, combine flour, sugar, lemon peel, vanilla, and chocolate liqueur. Make well in center of dough and, using a fork, blend in egg yolk and butter. Mix with fingertips until smooth. If mixture is too dry, add ¼ teaspoon more vanilla.

Liberally grease a 9-inch (3-inch high) springform pan and then remove sides. Place half of the dough on the bottom of the pan and form a ball. Place a piece of waxed paper on top of ball and evenly roll out pastry to edge of pan.

Remove waxed paper and bake pastry at 400°F for 6 to 8 minutes, until golden brown. Let cool.

Divide remaining half of dough into 3 equal parts and roll each part between pieces of waxed paper into a strip 2¼ inches wide by 9 inches long.

Carefully assemble springform with baked crust on bottom and line the sides of pan with unbaked pastry strips, overlapping ends.

Yield: 14-16 servings

Excerpt from a letter sent in 1785 by Thomas Jefferson—obviously, a truly great American—to John Adams:

The superiority of chocolate drink, both for health and nourishment, will soon give it the same preference over tea and coffee in America which it has in Spain.

CHOCOLATE FANTASY #29

Chocolate that glows in the dark . . . so you will never suffer during a blackout.

Rich with a kick! There is no better description for this pie.

LUSCIOUS CHOCOLATE BOURBON PIE

NANCY BISSELL—BERKELEY, CALIFORNIA

5 large eggs, separated
5 tablespoons sugar
½ cup bourbon
1 teaspoon vanilla
8 ounces unsweetened chocolate
9-inch prepared pie crust of your choice
lightly sweetened whipped cream (if desired)

Combine egg yolks and sugar and beat well. Add bourbon and vanilla. Set aside.

In a saucepan or double boiler, melt the chocolate over simmering water. Remove from heat.

Beat egg whites until soft peaks are formed. Add to egg yolk mixture. Mix in melted chocolate.

Pour filling into pie crust and refrigerate overnight.

If desired, top with lightly sweetened whipped cream just before serving.

Yield: 8-10 servings

There is no need to spend $25.00 a pound in a gourmet shop for truffles—a very "in" candy these days—when you can make these fantastic chocolates at home.

RASPBERRY TRUFFLES

ANN VAN DER MEERSCHE—EVERETT, WASHINGTON

8 ounces semisweet chocolate
6 tablespoons sweet butter or sweet margarine
½ cup seedless raspberry jam
3½ tablespoons raspberry liqueur or crème de cassis
cocoa powder

In a saucepan or double boiler melt chocolate and butter over simmering water. Remove from heat and stir in raspberry jam and crème de cassis.
Refrigerate until firm.
Shape into ¾-inch balls and roll in cocoa powder.
Store in a covered container in refrigerator.

Yield: approximately 4 dozen truffles

CHOCOLATE FANTASY #30

Chocolate exists . . . some fantasies do come true!

INDEX

CANDIES

CHEESECAKES

COOKIES

DRINKS

Chocolate Enchanting Shake 58
Chocolate Lustre 111
Mug o'the Morn' Chocolate Mocha Coffee 48

FRUITS

Chocolate-Strawberry Opulence a la Creme 122
Festive Fruit Salad for All Seasons 42
Peaches 'n' Chocolate Creme 100

PIES

Choco-Cream Cheese Pie 54
Chocolate Coconut Dream Pie 6
Chocolate Meringue Pie 115
Fudge Sundae Pie   35
Luscious Chocolate Bourbon Pie 137
Peanut Butter Pie 125

PUDDINGS AND MOUSSES

Chocolate Mint Bread Pudding 38
Chocolate Bread Pudding with Almond Cream Sauce 62
Chocolate Velvet 103
Cocomaretto Fantasy 126

AND CHOCO-CETRA

Chocolate Date Nut Bread 20
Chocolate Diablo Delight 80
Chocolate French Frosting 18
Chocolate Plus Fondue 120
Creamy Mocha Fudgie-Wudgies 84
Hot Fudge Sauce 92

ALPHABETICAL INDEX

Chocolate Peanut Butter Cheesecake 82
Chocolate Pecan Oatmeal Squares 56
Chocolate Peppermint Creams 10
Chocolate Plus Fondue 120
Chocolate, Prune, and Cognac Cake 50
Chocolate Raspberry Bars 86
Chocolate Raspberry Cake 130
Chocolate Silk Cup Cakes 33
Chocolate-Strawberry Opulence a la Creme 122
Chocolate Tortilla Torte 88
Chocolate Turtles 91
Chocolate Velvet 103
Chocolate Zucchini Cake 40
Cocoa-Cola Cake 12
Cocomaretto Fantasy 126
Congo Squares 9
Corn Flake Chocolate Squares 59
Creamy Mocha Fudgie-Wudgies 84
Fantastic Chocolate Layer Cake 104
Festive Fruit Salad for All Seasons 42
Fudge Sundae Pie 35
Hot Fudge Sauce 92
Lieselkuchen 44
Luscious Chocolate Bourbon Pie 137
Macadamia Mocha Cheesecake 108
Mashed Potato Chocolate Cake 16
Midnight Surprise 26
Mocha Brownies 66
Mug o'the Morn' Chocolate Mocha Coffee 48
Pattie's Never Fail Brownies 47

The chocolate chip cookie was invented in 1930 by Ruth Wakefield, the owner of the Toll House Restaurant in Whitman, Massachusetts. Since there were no ready-made chocolate chips at the time, she cut up a Nestlé semisweet chocolate bar and added the pieces to the cookie batter.

Thank you, Ruth!